SHOCKING PROFIT

CASH IN ON YOUR COMPANY'S HIDDEN VALUE, GROW LEADERS, AND SPARK A TRANSFORMATION THAT CHANGES EVERYTHING

TIMOTHY VAN MIEGHEM

SHOCKING PROFIT:
Cash In on Your Company's Hidden Value, Grow Leaders, and
Spark a Transformation That Changes Everything

What People Are Saying

"Tim Van Mieghem's 'Shocking Profit' is a masterclass in uncovering hidden value and driving ethical profit."
—Gino Wickman, Author of Traction & Shine, Creator of EOS®

"This book's an eye-opener. After 40 years as a global sales and marketing consultant, I was SHOCKED by Tim's examples of finding massive profits for clients, often right in plain sight."
—Orvel Ray Wilson, CSP, Co-author of Guerrilla Selling,
The Guerilla Group, https://guerrillagroup.com/

"A great roadmap for the due diligence owners should do consistently to unlock 'Shocking Profits' and capture the value for themselves."
—Mark Panico, Principal, Following Seas Business Consulting,
https://www.linkedin.com/in/mark-panico/

"Tim Van Mieghem delivers a powerful, practical roadmap for driving ethical growth and lasting success. A must-read for rising executives eager to create real value and for board members committed to helping companies thrive and prosper."
—Bob Hund, Operating Partner, HCI Equity Partners,
https://www.hciequity.com/

"Shocking Profit is a guide to cultivating awareness, spotting hidden opportunities, and transforming challenges into growth. If you want

to sharpen your vision as a leader and uncover profit that's hiding in your blind spots, this book is a must-read."
—Elaine Damschen, Former President,
Mainstream Electric, Heating, Cooling, & Plumbing,
www.ElaineDamschen.com, and Author of Made in Vietnam

"Shocking Profit is a treasure trove of insights on leadership and orga-nizational success. Tim Van Mieghem's practical steps for uncovering hidden value and fostering a problem-solving culture make this book invaluable for any organization."
—Eric Larson, Managing Partner, Tilia, https://tiliallc.com/

"The information is well presented and totally practical—ideas you can put to work right away. The book's structure—Awareness, Acceptance, and Action—offers a clear roadmap for leaders to unlock growth with-out massive investments. This is a book to visit over and over again."
—Gary Fretwell. #1 International Best Selling Author of Embrac-ing Retirement: Discovering Your Fulfilling Second Act, Speaker

"It is a must-read for any business owner who wants to create a self-suf-ficient business that can run without their everyday direction or a business that is ready to sell at any time. A must read for any business owner looking to get their time back and stop letting their business run them."
—Debi Corrie, Founder, Acumaxum, LLC, www.acumaxum.com

DEDICATION

With a mix of sadness and gratitude I dedicate this book to my partner and "brother from another mother," Doug Blanchard. Doug had my back, never let me (or anyone) outwork him, and he poured himself into our clients, our vision, and our team. His strength, wisdom, and infectious spirit were a source of inspiration to all who knew him.

Doug met the love of his life, Sue, when he was the quarterback for the Akron Zips. He continued to lead on and off the field. His legacy will live on not only through his children and grandchildren, but in all the people he mentored and supported. Doug's battle with cancer was fought with the same courage and determination that he brought to every aspect of his life.

This book stands as a testament to his enduring impact and the profound difference he made for so many.

Doug, I miss you and now get to carry on our mission.

Table of Contents

Introduction

WE CAN ALL SING THE opening tune. Jed Clampett ("Pa") goes from rags to riches by discovering a huge pool of oil in the swamp he owns in the hills of the Ozarks. "Black Gold ... Texas Tea ..." So, he loads up his truck and moves to Beverly... Hills, that is[1]. The rest is history (and comedy) for the Beverly Hillbillies.

In an instant, Jed's land went from being worth hundreds of dollars to hundreds of millions of dollars! He didn't create any value; he accidentally found the value that was already there.

And here's what I want to know: ***Who sold Jed that land?***

What if the previous owner had discovered the hidden value of the land *before* the sale? Did they think to assess their property and understand its true value before putting it on the market?

Indeed, the land was sold as farmland, not as an oil field—because they didn't know the potential they were literally standing on.

> **That owner must be kicking themselves!**

Sadly, this is a scenario I see play out all the time in my work with privately owned companies pondering the "what's next" for themselves, their businesses, and their families. My company, The ProAction

Group, has completed operational assignments for more than five hundred companies. 98% of the time we find at least one instance of hidden value that radically changes the profitability and value of the company—*without adding new equipment or more labor.*

In other words, many companies like yours are sitting on hidden value that doesn't need to be created but just needs to be enabled and uncovered! There's nothing to prevent you from getting access to the "oil" that's already there.

Then why do substantial companies with capable leadership miss these lucrative opportunities seemingly right under their noses? Two main reasons:

1. They get used to their current circumstances—the common trope "this is how we've always done it" comes to mind.

2. Most CEOs haven't looked at their business through the lens of investors like Private Equity firms, who do a deep-dive analysis of the company's capabilities against current market conditions and opportunities before they entertain a deal.

Here is the multi-million-dollar question: **Can you afford to sell your 100-million-dollar baby for $10 million?**

Is it possible you could be selling—or standing on—a metaphorical oil-rich land that could bring you Shocking Profit?

Perhaps you're not considering selling and you feel that your company is doing fine. I am here to tell you this: **Just because you may be doing better than some doesn't mean you're as good as you could be!** Even small improvements in your operations can compound into powerful advantages—the kind that make you tough to catch and harder to beat.

The punchline: *Would you rather be reaping the rewards of the hidden value in your company right now, or letting the next owner claim it and develop it for themselves?*

It's a safe bet you would choose to leverage more out of your company for the sake of the vision and dream you've worked so hard to achieve thus far.

This book is intended to help you do just that. What the PE (Private Equity) people know about leveraging hidden value and positioning a company for sale is what you need to know too—right now!

What the PE people know that you don't know

Private equity (PE) firms are in the business of identifying potential companies to invest in, grow, and in many cases, sell at a substantial profit. Their approach is finely tuned to gain a deep understanding of each target company's operations, so they have the information they need to refine valuations for competitive bidding—or to walk away from risky deals.

Thorough operational due diligence helps to ensure PE purchases are sound investments. This is where The ProAction Group comes in. For more than 30 years I have been fortunate enough to work with hundreds of business owners to help them:

- Identify the value hidden in their company.

- Quantify the financial and market impact the current state has on the company.

- Shed light on the risks of continuing on the current path.

- Build the plan and the budget to take action.

- Give the CEO what they need to make a responsible decision to move forward with what will often lead to transformational change.

When we're called in to conduct due diligence for our PE clients, we often see businesses that tell us they're doing "fine." What we discover might surprise you, but it is absolutely true: ***Within two days (sometimes two hours) of talking with the CEO and touring the operations, we have been able to observe quick-win changes that increase company profitability by 50 percent or more within six months!***

> **THIS is what you call shocking profit.**

Yes, you guessed it—there was Black Gold right under their feet they never realized existed. These are not unicorn situations; in fact, they're common. We detect warning signs that indicate inefficiencies, waste, or blocks to productivity. We sleuth all aspects of operations to uncover the root causes of the problems a company is experiencing, and indications of gaps in meeting customer needs. In so doing, we lay the foundation for quick wins as well as continuous improvement—and uncover the hidden value waiting to be leveraged.

Maybe I haven't "seen it all," but pretty close!

For years, this message has been swirling around in my head: *What if ANY company could identify that hidden value in their own operations? What would that mean to them?*

I know the answer because I see it all the time. They would:

- ▹ Position themselves competitively in the market
- ▹ Achieve higher levels of employee engagement
- ▹ Reinvigorate their dreams for the company and their personal lives
- ▹ Bank shocking profit!

Have you ever prepared your house for sale where you had to do repairs, update appliances, repaint, get it staged, etc.? When everything was completed, you said, "Wow, what a great house! Why am I selling it?" And maybe you even decided not to sell after all.

This is how I view your business. You may have hidden potential—bubbling crude—that you don't even know is there. You could uncover that value now instead of waiting for someone else to discover it.

These swirling messages finally convinced me that I had to do something about them. So, I wrote this book.

"SHOCKING PROFIT" represents the best of my knowledge and experience, as well as that of successful experts in the investor and private business ownership spaces.

The size of the prize

Investors want to see a company's overall potential financial reward or opportunity in a particular market—in other words, ***the size of the prize.***

What is YOUR size of the prize?

After an operational diligence assessment, I said to Joseph, owner of Magnum Manufacturing, a $50-million-dollar maker of industrial furniture, "We can do a project with you that will double the output you're currently getting on this line." He replied, "Why would I bother doing that when I can just buy more equipment and not have to spend all this time trying to get better?"

This is one of my favorite questions and an apt illustration of the theme of this book. I responded, "Right, Joseph, you could do that—but at what point does it end? For how long do you keep getting just half the capacity out of the equipment you buy? Are you waiting for your competition to sell under your costs and run you out of business because they've designed a more efficient approach?" Joseph, I am happy to report, did embrace the process and his team learned to get the full capacity of the equipment. (Joseph may have been testing me ...)

What he and many business owners often miss is the cumulative effect of small improvements: efficiencies in their manufacturing processes alone can enhance their position in the market. When you understand the value of your company, you'll stop the leakage that's slowing down your business. Can you think of a business (maybe one that rhymes with "Ballmart"?) that dominated an industry by being marginally better than their competition in many small ways?

Let me ask you this: If you were Jed Clampett and saw a pool of bubbling crude working its way along a field on your property, would you sell that land in a heartbeat and buy a home in Beverly Hills with a "cement pond" (a pool)—or walk back to the barn, doing things the way you've always done them?

For Joseph and Magnum Manufacturing, we achieved a positive result by opening his mind.

If you're still wondering about the size of the prize, consider these benefits:

- **Tactical = more profits.** When you have more productivity, efficiency, speed, and less waste, you're going to make more money and grow faster.

- **Strategic = positioning for the future.** What you do now will have a key impact on what you decide to do with the company (and your life) in the future, such as fulfilling a succession plan or selling. There's no time like the present to position your company for the highest possible value, especially if you decide to keep running it.

- **Big Picture Benefit = impact on lives.** It's simply a great way to live! When you work in a company whose mission is to bring out the best in its people, everyone's experience shifts from being a job to a mission, to a vocation they believe in. They're happy and engaged in their work and their lives at home. When your company is passionate about continuously doing your absolute best, you accomplish things you would never have accomplished otherwise. I'm talking about ethical—and joyful—profit!

Guide to mining the gems in this book

Whatever your company is facing, whether it's problem-solving, improvement efforts, scaling for greater profits, or positioning for exit, *Shocking Profit* is structured according to a fundamental, proven three-stage approach, *Awareness, Acceptance, and Action*—each stage necessary to guarantee success.

Section I: Awareness. Simple, clear ways to self-diagnose potential risk and waste in your current operations. Black Gold doesn't mine itself! Do the due diligence within your organization, based on the question: *What would we produce if every day looked like the best day?* Begin to build the blocks that pave the path to discovering your company's hidden value and converting it into higher profits. Any change effort is dead in the water without first building awareness of the problems and realizing the size of the prize for fixing them!

Section II: Acceptance. How to set the stage for a transformational improvement initiative. Moving from Awareness directly to Action stunts growth and prevents transformation. As Dale Carnegie once observed: "Someone convinced against their will is of the same opinion still." It starts with your leadership: how you become a champion of change for your company—building a compelling business case for change worth doing; and preparing your company with the strategic next steps to reach your desired future state.

Section III: Action. Taking purposeful action which not only mines hidden value, but also creates a problem-solving, self-improving organization. Through solid metrics, testing, and reviewing, you execute your improvement plan. You sustain your standardized process (the "virtuous cycle") to guide continuous improvement going forward with a strong team and problem-solving culture. The result? A workplace of happy employees who find meaning and satisfaction in their work, while you pursue exciting opportunities for your personal future—Shocking Profit Nirvana!

A word about ethical (joyful) profit

After graduating from Marquette University with a BS in Accounting, I took my first job at Arthur Andersen as an auditor. I'd chosen accounting because my dad was a CPA, and he loved his job. I loved my dad and was eager to follow in his footsteps. I didn't know when I walked into the office that first day that I would be in for a bit of a shock.

I had hardly settled into the first folder before I began to think, *Oh my God, this day is taking forever ... What time is it?* I looked at the clock: 8:30 am! By my fourth cup of coffee and the end of that first audit, I was committed to making a change.

Sincere hats off to the auditors out there—you're needed, it is important work! It just wasn't for me. I felt like I was checking other people's work with the purpose of pointing out where they screwed up. This was not the measure of my accomplishment, at least to me at the time. It clearly wasn't a good fit.

Originally, I had been attracted to Arthur Andersen because of their "Profit Improvement Practice," a specialized consulting service where my good friend, John Edwards, had a leadership role. I reached out to him and cajoled him into giving me a shot. I had some good computer skills and (it seems) decent skills of persuasion—I was given the chance to work on a project to help a company improve their freight sourcing.

Everything changed for me, and I was so grateful to John for going to bat for me. I felt I was actually helping people change how they operate, improve, and have a better time at their job. I didn't care if it was a Saturday or a Monday—both days were awesome, it was that much fun! I felt the same spirit as people who work for a cause they believe in, and I feel that way to this day.

> **My goal in professional life, and in this book, is to help companies get maximum profit in ethical, healthy, sustainable, and joyful ways, through using the resources, talent, and leadership skills already available to them.**

Every single company has substantial opportunities to improve. Many are hidden, and I'm going to show you how to mine and refine them. If you follow the ideas in this book, you stand to see real impact in stress levels, employee engagement, and positive financial indicators in six to eight weeks!

Shocking Hidden Value

"Unrecognized problems do not get solved! Undiscovered value does not get mined! Unseen visions do not get pursued!"
—Tim Van Mieghem

AS CAPTAIN KIRK DEMANDS MORE power for the Starship Enterprise, Chief Engineer Scotty, in his classic Scottish brogue, delivers the iconic line, "I'm givin' her all she's got, Captain!" Facing the impending doom of a Klingon Death Ray is not a good time to discover a capacity constraint, but fortunately for Captain Kirk and the rest of the USS Enterprise crew, crisis is miraculously averted, and the crew lives on for another episode[2].

For manufacturing firms, when customer fulfillment problems and past-due order issues arise, a CEO may act like Kirk and "ask for more power." When these problems occur and capacity appears constrained, new equipment, a bigger facility, new technology systems, more people, a new production line, etc., are all natural requests.

While these can be viable solutions, ***increasing capacity is costly, takes a long time to implement, and may not be necessary.*** Investing versus "throwing money at the problem" can be hard to distinguish.

Before you commit to adding more capital expenditure, you have to find the root causes of the current, persistent operational problems. And here is the exciting part: THIS is where the hidden value--the Black Gold—is found!

Identifying and addressing problems is THE way to unleash the potential of the company. Let me emphasize that this doesn't mean taking a defensive stance (*Let's wait for the problems to happen and then react*). Instead, it's a proactive and practical view that when we're in pursuit of a vision or strategy, problems WILL come up. The key is to **prospect for problems** so they can be addressed.

Section I is about claiming the value you have created! You realize that there could be more value in your company, right now, than you had ever thought. You look for the signs that will show most of your "oil" is still under the ground.

In this section, you will discover how to identify where that value is hiding, and how to assess and leverage it in these 6 areas.

1. **Chapter One** shares about workarounds and waste. *How hard are you making it for your people to do their jobs*—do they have to walk uphill into the wind on ice while carrying an anchor?

2. **Chapter Two** is about segmentation and pricing. *Where are you making money and where are you giving it back?* Where are you charging customers less than they're willing to pay?

3. **Chapter Three** focuses on velocity and throughput. *Can you increase the output of a plant, office, service location, or resource?* Hint, the real value in improving is not efficiency, it's velocity!

4. **Chapter Four** is about supply chain and sourcing. *How well do you make sure you have what you need, where you need it, and when you need it?* How well do you leverage your suppliers' resources?

5. **Chapter Five** shares about keeping score. *How well do you track and monitor the leading and lagging indicators that drive performance?*

6. **Chapter Six** guides you through risk reduction. *What risks, seen and hidden, drag down the value and stability of your company?*

Note: I'll be talking often about a concept called ***going to Gemba***, a Japanese term defined as "the real place." The concept represents Japanese management practices, specifically Toyota's Production System, that has been adopted globally as a cornerstone of Lean Management and continuous improvement. For me, going to Gemba means that leaders make it a practice to leave their offices and visit where the value is being created—the factory floor or other operational setting—to observe the workers and the jobs they're doing.

There is nothing like firsthand experience—engaging directly with employees who are closest to the processes—to gain a clear, unvarnished view that might not be visible from a distance. You'll see that in my work, and in just about everything I'm going to describe to you in this book, this practice is essential to uncovering hidden value, becoming the kind of leader people want to follow, and executing improvements that are measurable and sure to be game-changing!

Coming up: After this and the subsequent two sections of this book, I share the story of one of my favorite ProAction clients which illustrates the **Awareness**, **Acceptance**, and **Action** structure in real time.

(Real-Life Example)— Part 1: Awareness

IN 2021, THE COMPANY WAS struggling with a backlog of past due orders, quality, and on-time delivery. They lost Home Depot. Now Alpha had a new problem. Instead of over-due delivery, they lacked sufficient demand. Without new customers, the company would fold. Alpha was in danger of breaking loan covenants that could put them out of business. The fate of 100 families hung in the balance. In 2022, Bob Conrad was brought in as the turnaround CEO.

Scene 1: The Struggle. Awareness dawns.

On his first day, Bob walked into the office, his face set with determination. He gathered the team for a meeting. "Alright, everyone. We need to address the quality and delivery issues immediately. We're losing business, and if we don't turn this around, we'll all be looking for new jobs."

Kevin, the plant manager nodded. "I'm on it, Bob. I'll make sure every order is inspected before it goes out. We'll work seven days a week if we have to."

"That's the spirit, Kevin."

Kevin moved around the facility like a whirling dervish, addressing issues and fixing problems as they came up. The inspections improved quality and on-time delivery, but they still faced a lengthening list of past-due orders and increased scrap.

Bob called Kevin into his office for an update.

"Bob, we're working seven days a week, but past-dues keep growing. Can you tell sales to stop accepting orders?"

"I know, Kevin. We need to win back stores, locations, and shelf space, one by one. The sales team is staying close to our large customers, trying to maintain relationships. We're not accepting new orders until we're confident we can deliver on time. The VP of sales is working with the Buyer at Home Depot to find other sources until we get our act together."

Kevin replied, "Alright, Bob, we'll do whatever it takes."

Through brute force, Kevin and the team improved quality, and ramped up to 50,000 units a month—and they started winning back demand. Customers were ordering 60,000 to 70,000 units every month.

Kevin called out the elephant in the room. "Bob, we've got the demand, but we can only produce 50,000 units per month. We're already working as hard as we can."

Now what?

To be continued ...

CHAPTER ONE

What is Blocking Your Progress— Workarounds and Waste

ARE THERE "RUSTY, LEAKY PIPES" in your processes that are corroding and eroding your people's ability to serve customers well?

Many of the companies we work with have invested time and money into great operational systems. Yet they're completely unaware of the patching, jerry-rigging, and workarounds their people are using every single day to actually make those systems and processes work for them in real time.

"The Walkie Talkie Workaround." Genius Auto Parts is a national distributor with 160 national locations. The limo looked out of place in Jackson, Mississippi. Mike, the new CEO, was visiting branch locations across the country to meet his team and to take the pulse of their concerns. The store was clean, and the sweet smell of oiled parts filled the air. Mike walked up to the counter and introduced himself.

"It's good to meet you Joe," (his name was right there on his shirt). "I'm Mike, your new CEO." They sat down to chat, and Mike asked Joe what would make his job easier.

Without missing a beat, Joe responded, "Walkie talkies."

This was *not* the answer Mike was expecting, but he smiled and asked, "What would the walkie talkies do for you, Joe?"

"Well, just this morning a customer walked in looking for a muffler for a '73 Datsun. I looked it up on the computer. It showed we have the part, but I'm never sure about that—I don't trust the system to be right. And I don't want to promise a part to the customer if we don't actually have it!

"If we had walkie talkies, I could call Bob in the back to check the shelves. That way I can be sure the customer gets what he needs, and I don't have to leave any customers alone at the counter while I go hunting for it."

Joe's response made Mike cringe—probably like you are right now because you can see the underlying issue here! Mike was impressed with Joe's creative initiative to adapt to his situation and figure out how to serve his customers—the right thing to do in his position.

While we applaud Joe's can-do attitude, do we want him to work that hard just to do the most basic part of his job? It's one thing for an employee to figure out a way to satisfy a rare customer need. It's a whole other thing when they have to walk a city block to find a part.

Joe just wants to depend on an inventory system he can trust. If the system says you have it, you need to believe it. This may seem like a small deal, but multiply that interaction by the hundreds or thousands of decisions Joe and his coworkers need to make every day for that one store location. Then multiply that by 160 stores!

Workarounds cause more than one level of inefficiency. The impact goes way beyond the extra work of one person. When inventory (or, for that matter, any of your systems) is inaccurate or disconnected, you're forced to manage a complex system built on innovations that may be creative but inappropriate. Something that *should* happen automatically gets done manually instead. And sadly, we see this all too often.

When there is a lack of clarity, your people compensate. They buy extra inventory to cover what they're guessing they'll need—and you know how good people are at forecasting!

So, what does it mean to talk about rusty, leaky pipes in your company? It means that there are inefficiencies and gaps in your operational systems. You may have gotten by without noticing them or, as in Joe's example, worked around them—*and things seem to be fine or at least acceptable.* But know this: On so many far-reaching levels, systems that "leak" will steadily compromise processes, sap employee energy, and steal profits. This is the wrong kind of innovation. You'll see why in a moment.

Top 10 warning signs of leakage that cause wasted effort and routine workarounds

Here are some key signs that your organization may be spinning its wheels trying to circumvent a poor system. I call these "smelling salts"—the 18th-century ammonia concoction that was put under the nose of someone after they fainted or lost consciousness, in order to wake them up quickly[3].

You might find some of these quite specific and even petty—like an occasional drip in your bathroom faucet or slight dampness in your home's crawl space. Just like these household warning signs, leakage in your operations indicate a deeper issue that is inevitably going to fester and grow.

My goal here (and in subsequent chapters in Section I) is to "wake you up" to things you may not know or have not yet connected to a problem that is crying out to be solved. Awareness is the first step: See how these warning signs might apply to any systems you have in your company:

1. ***Your managers do the jobs of those who directly report*** to them and then complain that 1) they're too busy to take on anything more, or 2) their employees aren't doing their jobs right.

2. ***Inventory levels are growing but your sales or your on-time deliveries are not.*** Your operators start to run a scheduled order and find they don't have enough materials to finish.

3. ***There are no visible metrics.*** How do people know if they're winning? What does success look like?

4. ***Levels of labor costs exceed the labor required*** to run orders, often referred to as *labor utilization*. One of our clients was paying out 14,000 labor hours a month. We calculated they only needed about 3,500! Over 60% of their labor hours did not go to running saleable product; instead, those hours went to rework, producing scrap, waiting for a line to start up, sitting through downtime, and overstaffing.

5. ***You don't know the accuracy of your perpetual inventory system.*** Can you tell if it's inaccurate? How much excess and obsolete

inventory is there? How does your inventory reserve compare to actual excess and obsolete inventory?

6. **Variation.** Does the outcome of completing an order vary based on the shift, the facility, the supervisor or the team? Variation is bad.

7. ***Some employees and execs are regularly asking the warehouse manager how to find a specific item.*** Something's wrong with the systems if anyone above supervisor level is involved in day-to-day operations of this kind.

8. ***Stacks of boxes in the warehouse aisles.*** Unless the company has grown more than 20% in the last few months, this is NOT a space issue; it's a sign they have more inventory than they planned for. Very inefficient and potentially costly.

9. ***People complain that the system doesn't work.*** When they do, it is rarely the fault of the system. It is almost always the lack of data integrity. The systems work. Data hygiene is the issue.

10. ***Reports that people (employees, vendors, customers) are frustrated,*** flustered, exhausted, or volatile. People are noticing signs of stress: tension, infighting, blame-gaming, or avoiding accountability. Remember, there is a healthy stress that occurs when people are working to achieve a goal. "Unhealthy stress" signals that something is wrong—NOT a sign that people are just working hard or customers are just being difficult. People thrive when things are proceeding in a constructive manner.

As the leader of your company, your goal is to set up systems and processes that make it easy for good people like Joe to complete orders and provide services to your customers—without workarounds. The flip side is also true: You want to make it difficult to go *outside* the systems you've created—because they work.

> **Ninety percent of your work, your orders, or workstreams should flow through the system like Usain Bolt[4] nailing a 100-meter sprint!**

The prize is even bigger than this! When you plug that black hole of wasted effort, you serve your customers better ... and *you can leverage creativity and innovation because you're able to focus on high value-add topics which will lead to delighted customers, a new product, a competitive edge.* What is a surefire sap to creativity and innovation is having to focus on the everyday, routine, normal daily business activities that your systems were designed to handle.

Are workarounds ever tolerable? Yes, especially for rare work completed by a few people, or when you're developing a new process. This chart shows when workarounds are most appropriate:

Figure 1. Chart

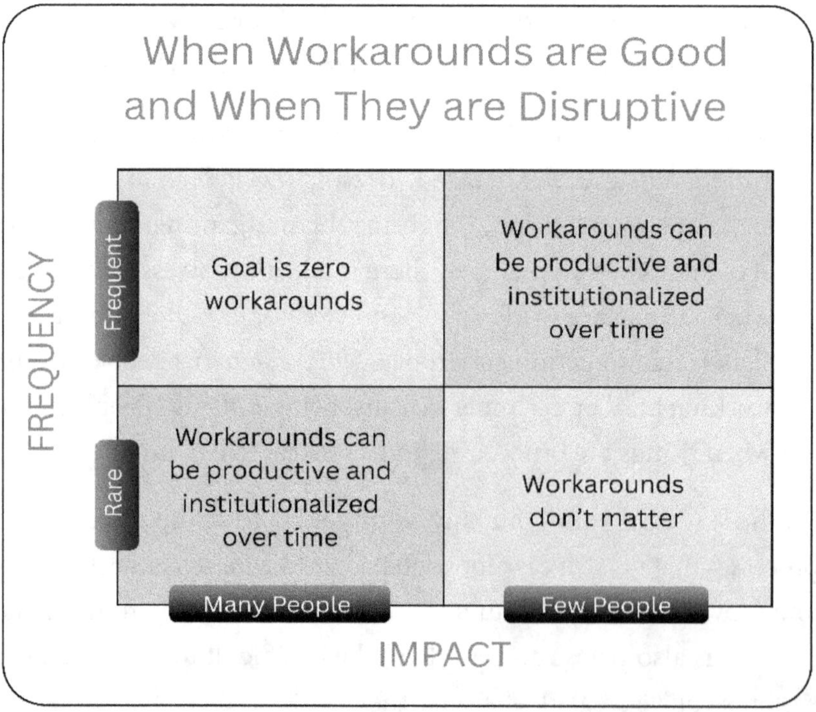

When Workarounds are Good and When They are Disruptive

FREQUENCY	Many People	Few People
Frequent	Goal is zero workarounds	Workarounds can be productive and institutionalized over time
Rare	Workarounds can be productive and institutionalized over time	Workarounds don't matter

IMPACT

What would it be like if the "Joe" in your company—an employee who is hard-working, cares about customer service and the company, and is creative with a can-do attitude—were freed up to really use their talents and initiative to contribute in more meaningful and productive ways (than begging for "walkie talkies")? Now, multiply your "Joes" to see whether or not the size of the prize is worth finding those leaks in your systems.

The current approach produces the results you get today—and those results can get better!

If you recognize any of the warning indicators I listed above, I have three pieces of great news for you:

1. Your company will continue to perform despite carrying the weight of inefficiencies on its shoulders. It's likely that doing things the way you're doing them now is getting results. Addressing an issue of leakage will simply take you to a new and better level, making everything flow more smoothly and easily, and giving your team the gift of bandwidth to focus on value-adding activities!
   Steve Bentson, a friend, colleague, and serial CEO, shared that we can "redesign the system; perhaps it was the process that was deranged."[5] (Steve Bentson | The ProAction Group)

2. Recognizing the symptoms is not a life sentence. You can and should address these symptoms, and I can assure you that there's a great chance you can do this with the resources you already have!

3. Unrecognized problems do not get addressed. So, congratulations—you have started the journey!
   "Leaks in the System." The hero of our story is an émigré from Greece who started a company in his kitchen that now produces

detergents made solely from common and safe ingredients. You could drink his laundry detergent or his window cleaner (not that you would want to but they're *that* safe!) The company has scaled rapidly into a multi-plant footprint with employees in five different states, making money even as he instituted a minimum wage in their factories years ahead of the market (he is a good man!)

However, as they're growing, so are their problems, causing customer complaints, and increasing stress and frustration in the front office as well as on the shop floor. Among some of the issues they face:

» Inventory levels have grown to historic highs, yet they struggle to fill orders.

» They go to produce an order and find they don't actually have the raw materials and packaging in stock.

» A customer will place an order, but they then don't have enough inventory to fill it. So they interrupt the work on the line to run the product their customer needs.

» The team spends their days expediting orders, feeling forced to check on everything themselves, instead of focusing on their regular responsibilities.

» Sales expresses frustration with Operations: "Why can't the factory just fill these orders? Don't they know how hard it was to land this customer?"

» Operations show frustration with Sales: "Why can't they tell us what they're going to sell? Can't we get a bit of a heads-up when we have a large order coming?"

The management team has tried many things—replaced plant managers, implemented a new computer system—yet nothing is working.

Why? Because they don't know what is behind the problems they're facing: *leaks in the system.*

So, they call us in. The first thing we do is investigate the current processes. We soon discover that each of the five locations has developed its own approach for using their system and running orders, so there is no consistency or coordination—some people don't even know how the system works.

Our goal is to help them set up their system to run 90% (remember Usain's 90%?) of their orders smoothly, without workarounds. We work with their teams to redesign their system, learn to use what they already have, and take back control so they can trust and leverage the system.

The results? In less than a year, this company:

» Increased output by 25% with existing workers and equipment;
» Cut lead times by 48%!;
» Kept and increased their customer base;
» Consolidated the five locations into three more efficient ones;
» Reduced voluntary turnover to almost zero; and
» Increased profits by over 40%!! (more than $3 million per year) Profits were SHOCKING!

Here is the moral of the story: **If you buy more expensive technology or equipment, you will just spend more money to NOT use a more expensive system.** Audit your process before investing in more capacity or even automating what you have.

By eliminating workarounds and enabling the team to leverage their current system, the company achieved all these improvements *without adding anything new—and with their existing team!*

Think what this could mean to your company! Let's find out by starting to address those signs of leakage.

Big picture upside

I often evaluate a business principle by considering how it would work in my personal life. Things that are true in one situation tend to be true in all situations. As we consider systems, processes and order, think about this: A morning routine at a house without order—how would it go?

"Bobby, where ARE your SHOES? We have to go!"
"Lizzy, where is your backpack?"
"Did you eat your breakfast, Sarah?"
"Mike, please tell me you're up! We're late!!! We have to go!"

Every morning is a challenge, always racing to make it to school and to work on time. Micromanaging every kid and every activity. Our stress and frustration are building and we're trying hard not to say something we'll regret later. Then we find out that someone forgot something, so do we make an extra trip to get it to them—or do we let them make do?

We come home in the evening to find out Bobby didn't lock the front door, or Lizzy let the cat out who's now disappeared. It is so stressful for everyone. Not a good way to conduct a day of learning or a day of serving.

How would this morning look if we had order, a system, and expectations which everyone understood? A special place for our shoes and backpacks where we can always find them. Certain days when Mike is responsible for making breakfast and Sarah checks backpacks. Everyone with an alarm clock that ensures they'll get up without any reminding and cajoling. A rule implemented that anyone who is late has to find another way to get to school.

Can you imagine how much easier life would be and, by the way, how responsible, self-directed, and proud of themselves the children would become?

That is what is possible at work. We will still work hard, but we follow clear systems and processes that support working efficiently and do work that will lead to satisfied customers, growing sales, good profits, and engaged employees!

What is blocking your progress? Bottom line

➡ Companies can be completely unaware of the patching, jerry-rigging, and workarounds their people are using every single day to make systems and processes actually work for them in real time. Working outside a good process ADDS work and STIFLES productivity!

➡ Ninety percent or more of your orders should flow through a normal process.

➡ Look for the warning signs that might indicate waste, and which can be fixed through improvements—without adding new equipment or systems and accomplished by your existing team!

CHAPTER TWO

How to Find 38% More Profit in an Hour or Less—Segmentation

AS INTOXICATING AS IT SOUNDS to find 38% more profit in an hour, we need to take a reality check before you jump in.

The unvarnished truth is that the decisions you make because of the ideas in this chapter may be hard and counterintuitive. The solutions will likely involve decisions such as raising prices on some customers, reducing inventory to increase sales, putting guardrails up, and saying *no* sometimes, and treating certain customers differently from others. We also have to work with the cost data we have, which is often not accurate.

Buckle up, friend. This segmentation analysis, fueled by real data, will give you great power. Wield it well.

While quite a bit of our focus in this book will be on work completed on the shop floor or in the field, in this chapter we're going to take a top-down approach and study the big picture.

The value gems I'm about to share rest on a foundation set by four principles:

1. **"One of these things is not like the other."** Some customers and Stock Keeping Units (SKUs) are more profitable and some less. They should be treated as such.

2. **Customers often won't tell us when they're willing to pay more.** Often this analysis shows that we determine our prices based on our costs, rather than what the market will bear.

3. **Poor processes cause symptoms that often have been "solved"** by throwing money, people and inventory at them. The symptoms persist.

4. **Data will not automatically convince people to do hard things** like increasing prices, saying no to a customer, or moving an item to "make to order". However, without data, these important decisions are never made.

Let's start with a story. Marcia, Marcia, Marcia ...

"Help! I'm Desperate!" At Wonder Widgets, Inc., Marcia in Sales gets a call from a loyal customer: "Marcia, I'm desperate, I'm out of this product! Is there any way you can get it to me tomorrow?"

"Sure," says Marcia, an attentive advocate for her clients, "let me check it out."

Marcia goes to the plant supervisor and says, "Hey, Customer Q needs this product tomorrow!" The supervisor immediately orders everybody to stop what they're doing. This means that they're interrupting the order of a top customer who's providing 85% of Wonder Widgets' profits!

They've just stopped everything to serve a small customer who is important to Marcia, but what does that mean for the large customer whose order just got postponed?

Well, this has been the standard operating procedure (SOP) at Wonder Widgets for about eight years, and the dominos are beginning to fall: Two large customers have left because of persistent delivery delays. Production costs have been creeping up, but no one knows why, and pricing hasn't kept pace. The sales team and production team are at each other's throats. Needless to say, in the plant the morale is low and turnover is high.

> **A company's bigger-picture productivity may not look good—because of bending over a dollar to pick up a penny.**

What we're talking about here is *segmentation: summarizing your business in terms of revenues, costs, inventory, SKUs/services, and number of transactions.* And doing it with a holistic, systemic approach which reveals the hidden value that will increase your profits in a most shocking way.

> **You could increase your profits by 38%—overnight!**

Then why isn't everybody doing this, you ask. My experience tells me, *they just don't know.* And it's my mission to make sure you do.

At the start of a client engagement, we will often ask the CEO this key question: "How much of your profit comes from your big items or services sold to your big customers? And they'll respond, "I don't know, maybe 80 percent?"

Here's a Shocking Profit truth: Most of the time it turns out to be over 100 percent—which leaves zero percent profit from their smaller customers. You guessed it: This means that they are literally losing money on smaller customers and smaller items—something like a systemic loss leader.

I think you and I agree that most CEOs would not intentionally decide to give smaller customers a lower price than their core customers, or to ask larger customers to underwrite your smaller customers! They're letting it happen because they don't know, and here are two main reasons why:

1. *They've never done a segmentation analysis* or a customer profitability analysis to identify what's happening and with which customers. Their whole business is functioning without the clarity that analyses and data can give.

2. *They let their customer relationships drive their business.* Don't get me wrong—this is a wonderful thing! I see CEOs with a tremendous amount of integrity who truly care about their customers. Their salespeople and managers have developed deep customer relationships, have their favorites, and will go to bat for them. Great! What they're missing is a clear approach to serving customers. You end up like a town with no stop signs or traffic lights—chaos!

Segmentation analysis helps you think about how you run your company. It's a way of breaking out the elements to make sure that you're prioritizing and treating your customers according to their segments and needs (and your profit goals); that your pricing approach is appropriate; and that you have sufficient investment in inventory.

These are the three keys:

#1: Profitability and priority
#2: Pricing
#3: Inventory/ Working capital

Identifying, analyzing, and understanding these three keys will tell you what you need to do—including the hard things like:

- *Recognizing that your business is not a monolith.* You have parts of the business which run quite differently from others. Treating them like they're all the same will lead to pain. (My right foot is in a bucket of water that is at 33 degrees, and my left foot is in a bucket of water that is 120 degrees. On average, I am comfortable ... but my right foot is going to get frostbitten and my left foot is going to get scalded!)

- *Issuing price increases* to smaller customers (who are less profitable).

- *Implementing guardrails on what SKUs* and services you offer, and how you offer them (lifecycle management).

Let's dive in ...

KEY #1:
Profitability and priority

To help prioritize profitably, ask yourself:

> *Are we following the dollars?*
> *How profitable are our customers?*
> *Which ones do we make money on and which are we subsidizing?*
> *Are we running our business to serve and protect our bread and butter?*

Operations/ Order fulfillment approach. Every business has a mix of relatively high-volume and relatively low-volume products and services (which I'll refer to as an SKU). As I mentioned, it's never a one-size-fits-all situation. Problems start when the company has chosen only one way to run their operation.

Are your company's products high-mix and low-volume, or low-mix and high-volume? When we ask this question, we always get an answer—and typically it is half right.

> **By nature, companies have BOTH high-mix, low-volume AND low-mix, high-volume products.**

High and low volume is a relative measure. Why is this important? Because you run a high-mix, low-volume operation differently than you run a low-mix, high-volume one!

Here's gold to be mined: You serve the customers that put the butter on your bread—the "A Customers." And you serve all your other customers to the extent that it doesn't impact those A Customers.

This is the power of setting priorities and treating each segment of your business on its own merits. This chart on segmentation analysis breaks it down for you.

Figure 2. Chart

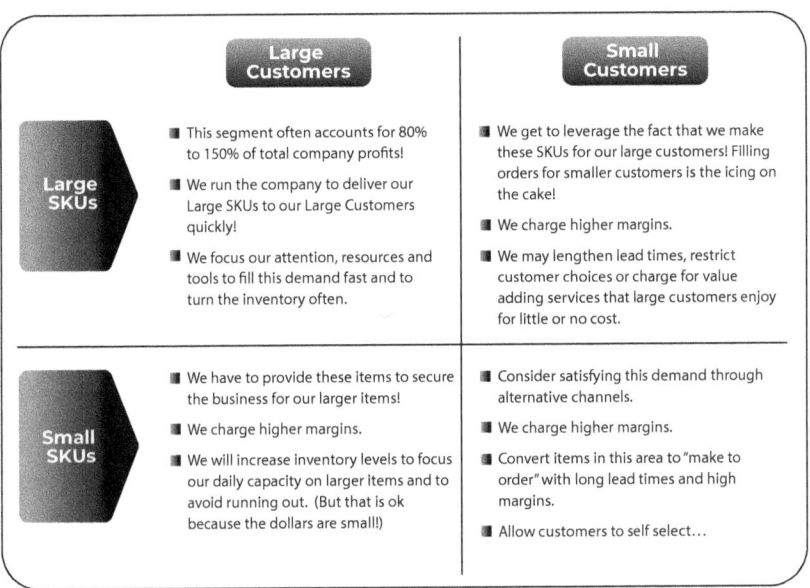

To illustrate how it can work, here's a quick story:

"All SKUs are not created equal." Chris runs a high-end upholstery manufacturing company, Home Haven Ltd. She is wrangling with a classy problem, and her frustration shows on her face. Her company has grown fairly dramatically and is now struggling to keep up with customer orders. Part of the struggle relates to a tight labor market—they are unable to attract and retain enough workers to keep up with demand, and she's anxious about the impact of increasing wages.

Chris asks us to review her operation and give our opinion on whether it would be healthy for the business to increase wages.

As part of our analysis, we segment her customers and the products (SKUs) and look at the profitability and activity in each segment. This is what we find:

- 86% of sales and gross profit come from 7% of her SKUs *(93% of her SKUs produce only 14% of sales and gross profit).*
- Similarly, over 85% of sales and gross profits come from a handful (10%) of their customers (A Customers).
- The next 90% of the customers only provide 15% (B customers).
- They manage all SKUs using the same planning approach.

Ah, the benefits of a bird's eye view! Armed with this data, Chris is now able to jump into a helicopter and fly above the day-to-day tasks related to serving customers—she can see clearly now!

Here is what this segmentation analysis leads to:

- Starting immediately, they have all the buyer-planners and schedulers focus their time and energy on the 7% of SKUs that drive their profitability. They work hard to keep inventory turnover high while satisfying customer demand.
- For 93% of their SKUs, they will keep three months of inventory on the shelf and refill their inventory levels when they drop below six weeks. They set this *kanban* system on autopilot. It's 14% of sales and 93% of the complexity. We build a visual-based trigger to make this routine.

- The plant is now empowered to run operations to satisfy B and C Customer demand in ways that do not impede serving the A Customers.

  » B and C Customer lead times are increased.
  » Price increases are levied on low-profit B and C Customers.
  » B and C Customers have to pay a premium if they want emergency service.

In the end, Chris did not need to hire more workers, invest in more equipment, add overtime or build a new facility to continue growing. She was no longer trying to fit 10 pounds of stuff in a five-pound bag. Rather than get a new bag, Chris focused on the first pound that provided 87% of her profits—and found out she had plenty of room!!

At this stage in the conversation about customer profitability, people will often go to the extreme and think about firing customers (maybe you were wondering how this would work?). Don't panic! The next section gives you many options to serve smaller customers without impinging on your ability to serve the customers who keep the lights on. Let's not make them walk the plank too quickly! Before taking drastic measures, ask yourself some important questions ...

Profitability priorities:
Five indicators that your company is leaking money

1. Are all your customers treated the same? Do you allow small customers to impact your ability to serve your key customers? Do you have terms, boundaries, and exceptions for those key customers who differ from smaller, less strategic customers? You may decide to give free freight, tight lead times, and value-added services to your A Customers. They're the ones who keep your lights on, so this could make sense.

2. Do you monitor margins by product and customer segment? The management team needs to have reports showing trends and variations in actual transactional prices, by customer and part/SKU segment.

3. Are margins on lower-volume SKUs and higher-volatility SKUs differentiated from high-volume or stable products? *Low volumes and high volatility drive higher costs.* Generally speaking, these items should have a higher margin than products that drive high levels of steady demand. Value is added when you provide the desired quantity of low volume and volatile parts to customers when and where they want them.

4. Does the executive team track and monitor SKU and customer segment margins? Smaller customers do not have the scale to evaluate other options that larger ones do. Design a policy or pricing approach at CEO/leadership level, which differentiates how you price different customer segments.

5. Are you experiencing break-ins which disrupt production schedules? When it comes to production schedules, many are cold and a few are frozen—schedules are set and then they change. If this happens often, it is a sign that you're not managing your demand planning well. And do customers have any skin in the game to avoid these expensive interruptions?

Recognize that break-ins exact a real cost to the company. I was once shocked to hear the cost a vendor would be charged by an automaker for shutting their line down for *one hour*—hundreds of thousands of dollars! For your plant, what is the value of one hour of production? It is probably more than you want to admit.

Look for the patterns. Especially if you have not segmented your business in the past, this exercise will show you where you work hard and make progress, and where you're on a treadmill staying in place. Then you'll know where you can eliminate the waste!

In Chapter Six, we'll cover the potential that your company either doesn't have good cost data or, perhaps more dangerously, is making decisions without knowing the real profitability of each product or service. We still complete the segmentation analysis—examining the revenues, quantities, and poor cost data of the business provides insights. And we bring in a cost accountant, incorporating their insights.

KEY #2: Pricing

In terms of pricing, ask yourself:

> *How effective is our pricing strategy? (In theory and in real life)*
> *Is our pricing based on the market? (Or do we price based on our costs?)*
> *How profitable are our different products and services? Which ones do we make money on, and which are we subsidizing?*
> *Are our pricing patterns working for our customers and us?*

At ProAction, we often kick off an assessment project in the boardroom talking with the executives. When we ask about their pricing strategy, they typically wax philosophical about how they study the market and consider the value add, proposition, and strategic importance of each type of customer.

Then when we look at the data and interview their teams, we find that actual decisions are not being informed at the leadership level, but being made in the trenches, based on the skills and perspectives of their salespeople. This news piques our interest. Clearly, executing a value-based pricing strategy buttressed by good market data and strong processes is going to win the day. However, *an internal logic to the pricing patterns* among different groups of customers and SKUs should be part of that. And these patterns need to guide ALL customer relationships (no matter who they are).

Figure 3. Pricing Chart – Margin to Customer Size / SKU Volume Relationship

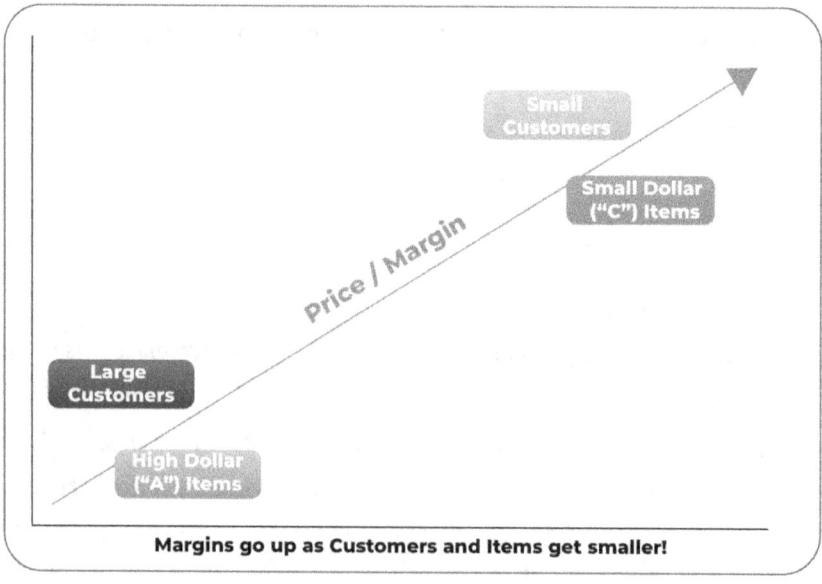

As customers get smaller and as the volume of the SKU or service gets smaller, margins should go up. Simple! In addition to basic margins, you can also impact margins and operations through customer management and SKU management.

Note: This is not a yes-or-no decision, and we're not jumping to the conclusion of firing customers. There are various effective ways to alter pricing, how you serve each customer, and how you manage the lifecycle of SKUs. Beyond pure price change, here are some examples:

- *Change the terms for smaller or less profitable customers* to allow you to serve them in a sustainable way. Some of my favorite options are:

  » Charge for freight.
  » Provide longer lead times.
  » Charge "break-in fees" for requesting expedited service (customers will think twice about asking you to prioritize their order if they have to pay extra to expedite a service).
  » Charge to maintain any custom products or inventory.
  » Charge for design work, quoting, or service.

- *Increase prices for smaller and more volatile items or services.* The more niche the product, the higher the margin! Extra credit: the more volatile the demand, the higher the margin. There is value in having items available for your customers whenever they need them. This value goes up as the demand for the items is more volatile.

- *Institute lifecycle management.* If you don't manage product/services end-of-life issues you will serve your inventory rather than it serving you!
  "Discounts Run Wild." ZZ Toy Company calls us in to solve a mystery: What is causing a double-digit gap between their gross and net sales? This company has hundreds of salespeople in a dozen regions. There is a companywide, executive-driven mandate to hold firm on pricing—which evidently isn't working.

With our best Sherlockian efforts, this is the issue we uncover: we find that salespeople are routinely providing discounts. They have good intentions and want to close the sale, but the executive team have developed their pricing strategy on sound principles and need their mandate to be carried out. The company's regional controllers are aware of the mandate but ignore enforcing it from a lack of conviction that it is truly in the best interest of the company.

With this intel in hand, we're able to design simple reports that track compliance and allow management to monitor pricing levels. This helps to bring everyone onto the same page, with the same message and expectations. Management's strategy is carried out throughout the company and net margins are increased by over 3 points. Starting with a 10% EBITDA margin, this strategy generates a 21% increase!

Caution: Emotions run high any time you consider price changes which put limits on some customers, and especially so if you decide to fire a customer. Be prepared to see inertia or pushback from your people around embracing these new ideas, which may make change difficult. Data and clarity—and courage—from leadership are required to address this issue (we will delve into this more in Section II).

Pricing: Five indicators that your company is leaking money through current pricing model(s)

1. When a price increase is decided, is the actual yield monitored?

Management must have access to sales history data in order to monitor performance. Companies that keep their sales history are able to retroactively track pricing change yield.

To perform due diligence, interview your managers and workers on how they address various functions and duties. Also look at history and actual numbers. This allows you to triangulate people's perception of how pricing is managed with real-life history.

2. Can a sales rep or inside salesperson change the price for an item based on their judgment? Salespeople only lose a portion of their commission if they reduce the price of an item. They stand to lose the entire commission, however, if they miss the sale. This factor can encourage personal goals and motivations to supersede company strategy and goals.

Establish proper controls that limit the ability for any salesperson or manager to provide a discount or price reduction outside of designed parameters. If these controls are not formal and discrete, there is likely a meaningful opportunity to investigate.

If your salespeople are compensated on revenue, then they should have little or no say on discounts/pricing. Margin-based commission structures often help align the interests of the salesperson and the company.

3. Are margins on projects or jobs tracked and compared to the quote? For custom projects and services, you need to provide a quote during the sales process. High-performing companies can show how completed projects and services compare to the original quote. You should be able to show what actions were taken to improve the quoting process based on actual performance.

4. Are you doing cost-plus pricing? There is opportunity to be found when "cost-plus" pricing plays a meaningful role in setting pricing levels. Alternatively, do you set prices on value delivered?

5. Are elastic and inelastic pricing not being evaluated? Retailers have found success in setting low prices on items that drive consumer behavior. If the grocery store sets a low price for milk, then customers flock to the store and they never check the price of snack items, for example. If you're not analyzing and tracking elasticity by part, then there is opportunity for improvement.

Segmentation allows you to evaluate pricing by the return each customer and SKU provides to the company. Starting by reviewing the data—the current situation/segmentation makeup allows you to focus your efforts on profitable customers and set terms and pricing for smaller/less profitable customers that results in them actually adding value to your company.

KEY #3: Inventory and working capital

To learn how inventory is a capital expenditure, and why it matters, ask yourself:

> *How much inventory do we need to run our company, given our demand patterns, lead times and capacity?*
> *How effectively do we collect from our customers and pay our vendors?*
> *What does our inventory level tell us about how we run the company?*
> *How can I Shock my Profit with better inventory management?*

When was the last time your CEO (which might mean ... YOU) sought board approval for additional capital investment in inventory?

My guess is ... *never.* No shame—inventory is not typically thought of as a capital expenditure. However, the consequence of this thinking is that mid-level clerks, planners, and schedulers can regularly make decisions to commit millions in inventory without executive review, approval, or even an evaluation of the business case! These decisions happen under the radar and are not given the same scrutiny as purchasing new equipment, making an acquisition, or launching a new product line.

Something is wrong with this picture, wouldn't you say?

I asked Bob, the CEO of a PE-owned company, how much he could spend on new items or projects without board approval. He shared that he could spend up to $50,000 at his discretion. We then looked at his inventory levels and found that his team had committed over $3 million to inventory *in excess* of the amount they really needed. Mic drop!

We often find that companies have two to three times the inventory level required to service their customer demand. The common motto is: *You can't sell from an empty cart.* While accurate, it often betrays an oversimplification and an endless justification for more inventory.

Excess inventory isn't the problem in and of itself—it's more like the canary in the coal mine. While it is good to improve working capital needs, *excess inventory tells us that other processes are likely increasing costs and reducing profitability!*

When companies have more inventory than they actually need to run their business, the excess inventory usually shows up in one of two areas:

- *High levels of base inventory or safety stock.* This relates to having more inventory of active items at any given time. For example, the company has the capacity to produce a typical order in three days, but they keep three weeks' worth in stock.

- *Excess and obsolete inventory.* This relates to inventory that no longer has meaningful demand. Time to clean out the closet!

A word about excess and obsolete inventory: Peter Drucker once said, "There is nothing worse than doing efficiently that which should not be done at all.[6]" Using your operation to produce product that customers won't buy for months is like driving a sports car in a school zone. Big opportunity cost, and a good amount of risk!

Either one of these "leaks" in inventory systems will drain a company of resources, build inertia to change, and require capital to fix.

Poor inventory management: Indicators that your company is leaking money through the management of inventory.

1. It is unclear who is being held accountable for inventory levels and determining which customers' and SKUs' inventory are made to stock and which are made to order.

It is too commonly believed that decisions are made with the view that inventory is free. It is not!

2. The company holds inventory that is sold only a few times per year. These might be highly seasonal or custom orders. Other than these, any inventory in excess of a week or so is likely waste. You should only have enough in stock to handle the next order. Decisions to maintain inventory levels for specialty orders like this should require executive review. Also consider that buyers often bring in more inventory than needed to hit quantity discount levels offered by suppliers.

3. Volatility does not impact the actual inventory level. As you segment demand, you also want to look at volume and volatility. A company should be able to fill orders for items with volatile or chaotic demand and needs to keep a higher number of days in stock. Keeping an average week's demand in stock doesn't work for items that might sell 1 or 100 in a week. When you find higher inventory levels for stable high-volume items, you'll get burned if you ignore volatility. Having appropriate levels of inventory for volatile items will help smooth out their impact on volatility.

4. The company does not benchmark lead times and inventory turns. This is one area where external benchmarks are helpful. If your company operates with industry-leading lead times and inventory turns, you're a truly high-performing company. If you lag in either or both areas, it is a clear sign that you have hidden value!

5. You pay suppliers faster than customers pay the company. In conjunction with other sourcing indicators, this can point to the need to develop and implement a sourcing strategy (more on this important topic in Chapter Four). In many industries it is common to have suppliers share in the real cost of capital in serving customers.

6. Days of sales outstanding (DSO) in accounts receivable is higher (worse) than industry norms. Is your DSO at or below target? After a sale is made and the customer is invoiced, a company has decided to rely on the customer's ability and habit to pay as negotiated on a timely basis. Companies that do not track DSO target levels or take longer to collect than other companies in their industry likely have an opportunity to improve.

For the right solutions, ask the right questions

So, let's say you and I are sitting across from each other (with our preferred beverage in hand), and we're looking over your segmentation data and analysis. What is your Segmentation Summary going to look like, and how are you going to use it?

This is the data analysis I'm going to walk you through:

1. **Have your summary** of sales, cost of goods sold, the number of SKUs, the number of customers, the number of transactions, and the investment in inventory for:

   » Large SKUs (A Items) sold to Large Customers
   » Large SKUs (A Items) sold to Small Customers
   » Small SKUs (B and C Items) sold to Large Customers
   » Small SKUs (B and C Items) sold to Small Customers

2. **Calculate the total operating profit** contributed by large SKUs sold to large customers as a percentage of the total. If it is around 80% you're a high performer! Some companies have more than 100% of their profits coming from large SKUs sold to large customers.

3. **Age your inventory.** Aging your inventory means that you calculate how many days, weeks or years of inventory you have on hand, based on the typical rate of consumption or sale. For example, if you use 100 pounds of salt in a day and you have 10,000 pounds in inventory, then you have 100 days on hand.

» Calculate "excess and obsolete" inventory. How much inventory do you have with no demand? How much do you have that will take more than one year to sell?

» Summarize the number of days of inventory on hand for stable and for volatile products.

With these numbers, you're going to complete your one-page Segmentation Summary. These are the questions you'll want to ask, and answer:

1. *Do we subsidize some customers and/or charge higher margins for smaller customers/SKUs?(Meaning, it costs us more to support them / provide this service/produce and therefore our margins are smaller.)*

2. *What degree of discretion do salespeople have to give discounts or offer a different price?*

3. *How do we differentiate the way we handle freight, value-added services, lead times, break-ins, and similar issues for A Customers versus B and C Customers?*

4. *When do we know what we will actually run in the plant or facility today—a week ahead of time, yesterday, or sometime today?*

5. *How do our Days of Sales Outstanding (DSO) compare to our industry? How do our terms with customers compare to our terms with our suppliers?*

Big picture upside

Think of this like education. Some people are visual learners, some auditory, others learn by doing (kinesthetic). Some need to learn in a group and some are better at doing it on their own.

Can you imagine the pain and lost productivity if we forced all children to learn the same way? I can speak for myself on this one: I was a C/D average student in grade school. My parents got comfortable with the idea that this was just the way it was going to be. They didn't pressure me or make me feel bad. Then in 5th grade, Mrs. Holmbo introduced "Team Time." We did projects and learned as a team. It was like a light switch flipped on for me. I may not have become an "all-A" student, but my grades did go up from then on!

When we're able to teach someone in the way they learn best, they stay engaged and they truly learn. Realizing she had "segments" of students who learned differently opened up a new world for all those lucky enough to have Mrs. Holmbo as a teacher.

When you design the approach to manage your various segments of products and customers, you're able to be surgical and granular, using a combination of data and measure as a 360-degree approach. You start by getting curious about the segments of the business, and do the work of compiling your Segmentation Summary, and *teach* your team its meaning and value so it can go to work for you.

By simply understanding the real segments of their business and where they made money and where they gave it back, these companies whose stories I share added over 38% in profitability, eliminated late orders, cut inventory (often in half), and virtually vaporized the operation of day-to-day chaos and stress.

38% more profit in an hour or less: Bottom line

➡ Summarize your business in terms of revenues, costs, inventory, SKUs/services and number of transactions (segmentation), with a holistic, systemic approach which reveals the hidden value that will increase your profits in a most shocking way.

➡ Your company could be finding value levers by:

   ✳ Treating each business segment on its own merits (segmentation)

   ✳ Knowing where you're making money and where you're subsidizing your product/service (pricing and segmentation)

   ✳ Realizing your inventory is a capital investment (inventory and working capital)

➡ For the right solutions, ask the right questions to create a holistic Segmentation Summary.

CHAPTER THREE

The Need for Speed—Mining Hidden Value for High ROI

Operational efficiency is a game of inches

COMPANIES THAT ARE EVEN MARGINALLY better than their competition can steal market share. In other words, even modest improvements to your existing processes will give you a celebration-worthy competitive advantage!

Here's a dramatic truth about what we do for our clients: We put less focus on improving how the company adds value to their customers—*we focus first on NOT doing things that do NOT add value.*

Lean manufacturing principles apply here—maximizing productivity while minimizing waste within a manufacturing operation. The result is getting clarity on what adds value to your business (possibly hidden in plain sight) and what does not (and is leaking money).

In this chapter we're going to *identify the gap between your current state and the full value which your company is already built to deliver*! In other words, what is your real capacity?

Speed of execution is extremely important for business momentum. A hidden opportunity can be found in looking at how your operational processes can work faster in serving the customer. Speed on its own implies moving fast. Velocity adds the concept of direction. Order fulfillment is a worthy north star.

This is what the PE people know—and it applies to any business that wants to do better than "just fine, thank you."

> **It's not about efficiency, it's about velocity!**

Let me be clear when I talk about speed vs. efficiency. It is not to say efficiencies are unimportant; it's that, in my experience, we can be inefficient and still get through the day, or the quarter ... or several years. But are our efforts increasing profitability?

What we're suggesting here is "velocity," the measure of the rate at which a process delivers its business objectives; how long it takes to achieve certain milestones; and the amount of work completed in a given time—the kinds of improvements that can translate into shocking profits!

Improving velocity means to *accelerate the actionable output* of a plant, service location, supply chain, or other operation with existing resources (most efficient) or additional resources (most costly).

> **When you can have 10–30% more throughput in the same organization with the same overhead, you are printing money!**

Increased velocity leads to:

- *Shorter lead times.* With an effective throughput process, everything takes less time and causes fewer workarounds and errors.

- *Outsized increases in profitability.* The faster you fill orders the more you're selling with your existing overhead in place.

- *Reliance on process.* A sustained increase in velocity requires ensuring the processes are efficient and effective—and then, consistently following them.

- *Depending less on forecasts and more on visibility.* In some cases this allows you to convert business from a make-to-stock approach (which requires you to rely on forecasts) to a make-to-order schedule. The benefits of minimizing your dependence on forecasts (which are always wrong to some degree) can be substantial!

- *Setting aside time to improve.* Continuous improvement processes require time. As you enhance your ability to fill orders in less time, you can shut lines down and run Kaizen events or improvement projects. This downtime can also be used to maintain equipment, train your teams and recharge your batteries. Speaking of your team, knowing they can rely on systems, accountability, and support from their superiors makes for happier employees!

Let's take a look at how this can work.

"Give us eight weeks and you'll have throughput!" The Fishy Business Company sold frozen salmon steaks in a sprawling plant in northern Washington. The sales team landed both Sam's Club and Costco in the same quarter, which doubled their sales! The celebration was short-lived as they ran into a classy, but thorny problem.

April, the president, told us, "We're working 24/7 and shipping record amounts of salmon—on pace to ship $14,000,000 for the year. The bad news is that we aren't even *close* to filling the new orders from the box stores. If we don't get to twenty million, and soon, we stand to lose both those customers!"

They had considered their options: They were using all the space available. They could build a new plant, but that would take more than a year and cost millions. Outsourcing would cut their already-slim margins and compromise quality control. Earl, the CEO, was feeling the pinch (closing in on desperation) because high-interest debt service put them in a precarious position—if they lost these accounts, they might lose the company.

April and Earl called us in to study their operations and see if they could fit enough new equipment into the current plant to get the volume they needed out the door. As we entered the plant on Monday, the nephew of the founder, George, who had grown up working at Fishy Business, met us at the door: "You're not going to find anything much. This company is running like a well-oiled machine." Okay ...!

The next day, we went to April and reported: "Give us eight weeks and you'll have your 40%. *No new equipment, no new people.*" When we showed Earl the numbers, he was shocked, particularly about this neat little statistic: Currently, salmon coming into the plant would leave as frozen, packaged salmon steak 36 hours later. We showed them it could be done in eight hours!

What was the basis of our big promise? There were lots of small factors, but the biggest ones were hiding in plain sight. Based on the very indicators you'll read about soon, we could instantly see that they were using only a portion of their capacity.

Here are the results and impact:

- Increasing shipments (and therefore sales) by 40% with a net reduction of 10% labor costs and a modest increase in overheads (additional supervision)
- Adding 40% growth without new equipment
- Reducing the work week from seven to five days (giving the workers their weekends back!)
- Standardizing the processes for each operation, making it easy to cross-train people and realize consistent performance on every shift
- Engaging the operators and supervisors in designing the new system. They now are able to take ownership of their areas.
- Increasing the value of the company by over $40 million in eight weeks

We took waste out of the system, made it easier for the operators to do their job, enabled the company to predict what should be accomplished each day, engaged the employees in new ways, and satisfied the customer demand without committing major new capital.

This is why you study velocity!

Top Ten Questions to ask to find hidden value

If you're not taking advantage of your operational processes to the max, it's like you're driving your Porsche engine in first gear on the expressway—grinding your gears and straining your engine! Eventually, something's gotta give, and in my experience, it always does.

Rather than seeing these indicators as an indictment, I see this as a fun place to be—like Christmas morning looking forward to presents and gift giving, especially the ones hidden under the tree that you hadn't spotted before!

Finding hidden value has you discovering and gaining awareness— and not trying to solve anything yet. You simply want to understand where you are. Be curious! DO NOT feel the need to address any issues at this point. DO ask yourself questions like these:

1. Have you defined capacity? If the company does not have a clear understanding of their real capacity, then they don't have a star to navigate by. The best answer is to calculate capacity based on running your lines at the designed speed for the entire day, with no downtime and no quality rejects.

Alternatively, you might estimate capacity by looking at the best day, the best facility, the best team, and extrapolate what they accomplish. Key question: *What would we produce if every day looked like the best day?*

2. How are you doing with late deliveries and/or past-due back orders? Sometimes poor customer service can actually be attributed to a lack of capacity—you simply cannot produce what your customers demand *when they want it;* you're not producing at the rate your customers require.

Late deliveries and missed deadlines may not be an indicator that the company is running slower than it could, but it shows you have a reason to find out!

3. Are your cycle times and lead times doing the job? The Waste Ratio is when there is a meaningful gap between the time it takes to fill an order and how long it takes to do the work without delays, there is an opportunity to speed it all up.

> **Top salesperson Patrick wonders why it takes three weeks** to get credit approval after he signs on a new client. He decides to walk through the entire process of one credit application IF there aren't any delays, and finds that *it takes 45 minutes—over three weeks that equals 30,240 minutes.* Thus, when you set aside all the waste and delay, their waste ratio, the ratio of value-added time to total time, is .14% (0.0014)! Therefore, looking into this process further enabled the company to cut three weeks out of their customer onboarding process. And their credit team had the capacity to handle significantly more volume.

4. Are inboxes regularly stuffed with work-in-progress (WIP) issues? When the lead time is greater than the cycle time, you will find things waiting to be worked on—plans sitting in the engineer's inbox; material waiting in front of an operation; people standing in line waiting for the next clerk. When we tour any factory or office, we look for WIP in front of machines, in warehouses, or in those inboxes. Any of these can indicate an imbalance in the lines and processes; bringing these into balance leads to cost, service level, inventory, and lead-time improvements.

5. Can you predict a good outcome? If you're 100% accurate in predicting that you're going to hit 30% of your goal for today, that is not a good outcome—your system isn't stable. You want to reach your targeted goals at least 90% of the time. Stability in velocity is tracked using a *closed-loop system*—a self-regulating system that continuously monitors and adjusts its output based on feedback, allowing you to check your results and alter course to increase speed of production. We'll explore the importance of closed-loop systems to your entire company in more detail later in the book.

6. What is the variation by shift, team, season, line, supervisor? Here is the gold to be mined: If one team, one worker, one line, one branch, one facility, or one salesperson demonstrates a notable level of performance, you may consider it possible for all to replicate those results (adjusting for product mix). You'll see a beautiful example of this situation in Chapter Nine.

7. Are you experiencing scrap, (external) field failures or warranty costs? Scrap is a double whammy. Not only do you have to discard finished work product, you have to write off the efforts, AND you'll have to re-do the item to fulfill the order. Adding to the pain, internal scrap leads to external issues. A surefire warning sign of value to be unearthed could be more failures than usual in the field or warranty claims.

The flip side is that any reduction in scrap creates capacity—if you stop making items you have to throw away (or process their return by the customer), you can use the time to make saleable items! These areas are the most fundamental types of waste to observe:

- *Defects:* Errors in products that necessitate rework or scrapping

- *Overproduction:* Producing more than is required leading to unnecessary inventory and increased costs

- *Inventory:* Holding excess raw materials, WIPs or finished goods that tie up capital without adding immediate value

- *Transportation:* Unnecessary movement of products or materials that increases handling costs and delays delivery

- *Waiting:* Idle time when resources are unproductive due to delays in the production process

- *Motion:* Unnecessary movement of people or equipment that does not add value, leading to inefficiencies as well as potential safety risks

- *Extra Processing:* Performing additional, non-essential work that does not enhance the final product for the customer

Individually, these can be identified and quantified for focused improvement efforts.

Collectively, they're the cornerstone of any operational excellence initiative to enhance profits, service, and morale!

8. How are you doing with production delays and downtime? As you work to fill customer demand, you want to be able to complete your work *when it needs to be done.* If there is a delay because a machine is down, a computer system isn't working, or you're waiting on inputs to your process, you're stalled!

Worse than that, if you're concerned that machines or processes won't work when you need them to, you will be forced to build ahead. If you're keeping inventory lean, then when you flip the switch to start production, it had better work! Can you imagine how different life would be if lights turned on at the flip of a switch 80% of the time?

9. Is line speed controlled and set to match customer demand? Are you on top of your line speed? Line speed needs to be measured and controlled. Too often the proper speed for a line or an activity is not clear. How long should it take for engineering to complete a design? What speed should this machine be able to run at?

Another scenario is slowing down the operation because you don't have enough work. This is a dangerous path. "Takt time" is a term that refers to the pace at which you need to produce products or services to meet customer demand (the goal is to match production with demand precisely). The beautiful thing about defining your takt time is that it then tells you the speed at which each operation needs to run, and it is based on actually filling demand.

10. Stress in the ranks or the C-Suite? As we mentioned in *Chapter Two* (and which will undoubtedly come up in some form again!), stress may be the most telling indicator of all. Pressure to meet a deadline amid chaos often leads to constricted thinking. Anxiety and stress cause people to lose creativity and their ability to make good judgments. Chaos breeds chaos. Conversely, engaged thought can speed up results dramatically.

You still might be wondering if any of this is worth it. In other words, *what is the size of your prize?* Many companies don't see a reason to look at their operation and consider, *could it be better?* Well, let me offer some food for thought.

A CEO got paid about $60 million for the sale of his company. Nice, right? It's a company he started from scratch and obviously did very well. However, when we did due diligence on this company for our PE client, we calculated the company's profitability. Had he addressed the issues we identified in our assessment, his payout would have been closer to $90 million—almost 50% more!

If only he'd known ...

Three keys to open the throttle on your need for speed

You already may have identified some indicators in your company, and there are likely some hidden goodies yet to be discovered. Any or all of these may offer opportunities for improvement that you can take to the bank! See, isn't it fun? What's next?

KEY # 1:
Operational diligence

Do the numbers:

- Look at production by worker, team, operation, plant, facility, shift, supervisor. Look for variation. Explore what prevents you from consistently hitting demonstrated peaks.

- Determine if the company's "perfect order" metric is above 97%.

- Review uptime versus downtime performance—how often does a patient scheduled for an MRI have to wait because the machine is down? Or how often does the internet go down and halt work for support teams or order processing? How often do you go to run a line and find equipment is causing delays?

- Calculate how many, if any, past-due backlogs of sales you have. In other words, how many orders exist where the customer would like delivery already?

- Find out if first-pass yield is measured and near 100%.

Make observations like these:

- Are there line-side metrics that provide clarity on what success looks like for the day, for every hour?

- Is there dust on any inventory?

- Is there any unplanned downtime?

- Is preventative maintenance (PMs) planned?

- Do operators have control of line speed?

- Does your WIP inventory equate to more than one shift of production?

- Are people standing around or inactive, or, just as telling, are people always busy?

- Are people frantic?

- Are the supervisors supervising? Is management on the floor or where the work is being done?

Measure production against what you planned

What do you do if you find out that you're operating at 70% speed, not 100%? What's happening here is your velocity is off—you're trudging uphill against the wind, and it's making life tough for your people.

One specific metric you want to pay attention to is *measuring production versus what you planned*. Also known as "schedule attainment," you're measuring how closely actual production aligns with the scheduled targets. This exercise holds true whether we're talking about a factory worker producing a product on a line, engineer producing a new design, sales manager doing quotes, author getting chapters done on their book (that would be me ...). It's all about producing something and getting it done according to plan.

When we work with companies that want to increase output, here's what we do:

1. *Calculate a baseline of the speed at which customers are demanding* the product or service (takt time). Let's say we want to increase by 30% to meet customers' demand. We look at what 30% means in terms of the number of units that need to go through the plant every minute (or whatever measure is appropriate for the company).

2. *Look at every single operation in the company* in terms of operating at that speed. We often find that many or most are operating at varying speeds, faster, or slower. We go to each operator and ask, "Can it operate at x speed?" If not, we would need more capacity, a second machine, etc. Or there's plenty of capacity that hasn't been utilized.

3. ***Set every operator to operate at the same speed.*** This means everyone is working in concert toward the same goal at the same time. It seems simple, so why isn't every company going full throttle?

The answer is that there are hundreds of things every day on every line that offer a possibility to improve—and they are not always obvious! Even the best companies and best people can squander their operational potential. You are not alone if this gives you anxiety.

We invite Fishy Business back to help illustrate:

"It's Always Been Medium!" Toward our goal to find an additional forty percent output in all their operations, we started measuring production. Janice, the plant manager, was walking us through the plant when we came up to the slicing machine, the most complicated machine in their factory. Here's how the conversation went:

Us: "Is this machine a bottleneck?"

Janice: "Yes, it is."

Us: "Does it run at more than one speed?"

Janice: "Oh yes (proudly), it's a multispeed machine."

Us: "What speed do you run it at?"

We see the blood drain from her face. "Um ... medium."

We reply gently, "Have you tried fast?"

Janice (sheepishly): "Um ... no. That's the speed I was trained on."

It sounds obvious, doesn't it? Well, Janice had learned how to run the plant from the guy who ran it for thirty years before her—this was how she was trained and how she'd run the machine ever since. It worked at medium; they had never needed to test it.

That very weekend Janice and a supervisor came in and tested the machine at the faster speeds. And it worked. Perfectly—forty percent faster. This was one of eight problem spots in the line, but it was the easiest to fix and had a happy outcome.

Amazing and profitable solutions can be as plain as the nose on your face or the field you're standing on!

KEY # 3:
Prospect and mine the hidden value

In the course of doing your operational due diligence, exciting questions may arise about what to do with all this hidden value that's revealing itself, such as:

> *Can we sustain our "new" leaner operations processes, as well as increase sales?*
> *Can we consider budgeting operational improvements?*
> *Can we afford to raise wages or hire more people? If so, how do we gauge that?*

Excellent questions!

Let me offer some considerations about the relationship between velocity and profitability, using the example of jobs and wages.

There is a way to look at the math with the holistic view of adding capacity to meet those increased sales opportunities—and there's a way NOT to do it. I've seen companies miss million-dollar contracts because they refused to spend an extra two to three dollars an hour (maybe another $100,000 a year) in wages. One CEO refused to go beyond adding a certain number of employees because he might be on the hook for providing insurance for all of his people.

Here's the miscalculation: In this case, he *literally* turned away customers so he wouldn't have to pay insurance! There could be a lot of factors involved here, like greed or fear. But here's the Shocking Profit point: Most often, it's an **inability to look at the business as a whole to gauge the ROI of increased wages or jobs that would create greater profitability.** We circle back to "just fine, thank you!" versus going for ethical profit and success.

> **When is it smart and when is it foolhardy to increase capacity? Let the numbers help you make that decision.**

When a leader truly understands how they make money, they will set wages to attract capable workers. Balancing improvements in productivity, velocity and sales growth with wage increases shifted the direction. *Providing a 20% wage increase enabled a 40% increase in profitability for this company.* Note: We're using wage increases here; other benefits might be retention, a more pleasing work environment, shift options, engagement, and other factors.

Big picture upside

Sir Roger Bannister was a runner and a bit of a loner. He did not follow the latest coaching trends and had his own approach to training. In 1954 he was the first person to run a mile in less than four minutes[7]. For decades, this goal was unattainable even with a worldwide focus. However, once Roger showed the way, another runner broke that same barrier in months. In the next 50 years thousands of runners joined them.

It is easy to understand how a company can become convinced that they're running at capacity, or as well as they could be. As the Fishy Business Company demonstrates, there is a major prize for making incremental improvements. In the prior chapter on segmentation, we explored how following the data and looking at actual results can highlight patterns and truths that will change your results. This chapter has a similar note: By understanding your actual capacity without constraints, you can expand your thinking and understand the true value of your company. You can find the oil under your farmland!

The need for speed:
Bottom line

➡ Companies even marginally better than their competitors can steal market share. Even modest improvements to your existing processes will give you a celebration-worthy competitive edge.

➡ Improving velocity refers to accelerating the actionable output of a plant or operation with existing resources (most efficient) or additional resources (most costly).

➡ Do operational due diligence to identify what in your operations prevents you from consistently hitting peak performance. Measure production against what you planned (schedule attainment—always leading with the customer's needs being met).

CHAPTER FOUR

Taming the Giant —Supply Chain and Sourcing

CONSIDER THIS: NO MATTER THE size of your company—even if you're Google or Amazon—the resources and capabilities of your suppliers dwarf your own! You can go far beyond negotiating price, quality, and delivery to leverage those resources. Learning to wield your suppliers' capacity and their supply chain will reveal hidden value that will set you apart. Taming the Giant requires that you develop trust with the right suppliers. It is a rare thing to do and beautiful when done right.

> **The company that leverages supplier relationships gets the competitive edge, every time!**

We're going to explore how to evaluate the hidden potential in your supply chain in four areas:

1. **Sourcing.** How well do you pick your suppliers and offer competitive and value-adding terms?

2. **Supply chain design.** How well designed is your distribution, office, and manufacturing footprint?

3. **Supply chain management.** How well do you source the right materials and services at the right time from the right supplier? How well do you manage the supply to meet your demand? How well do you plan demand, plan the supply and predict the outcomes?

4. **Logistics and warehouse management.** How well do you move goods and services accurately and efficiently?

Does your farmland cover a swamp, fertile ground, or an oil field? How do you know? What does "good" look like, not to mention "great"? Let's start with the questions you'll want to ask to see if you're missing some Black Gold opportunities.

#1 SOURCING:
Choosing the best suppliers and negotiating great agreements

For many manufacturing and distribution companies, the cost of purchased goods and services is 40–80 percent of the cost of goods sold, which can represent millions and millions of dollars in purchases a year. Yet in many cases, relatively low-level clerks, engineers, and untrained buyers are the ones deciding which suppliers to buy from—and negotiating contracts based only on pricing, quantity, and delivery! Sometimes the CEO is personally involved in selecting supplier relationships. In both scenarios, they're likely missing some bigger-picture benefits to the company.

You may already know, or you're soon to find out, how many other aspects of supplier selection, negotiations and management are involved, how many risks there are for leaking profits, and—the best news—*how many opportunities can be mined for tremendous improvements in operations and Income (for some this might be measured as Earnings before interest, taxes, depreciation and amortization, or EBITDA).*

Here are eight areas to diagnose leakage and find opportunities in your sourcing process. Ask yourself:

1. Do you have a defined and documented sourcing strategy?

In Chapter Two we touched on poor or no sourcing strategy as a warning sign that a company is leaking money—let's expand on this idea. If a company does not have documented sourcing strategies, it's an indicator there is significant opportunity to better utilize their leverage with suppliers. Remember our friend Bob, CEO of a company who found that his team had committed over $3 million to inventory in excess of what they needed? It would have been difficult to fall into that trap if they had had a clear, documented sourcing strategy!

Relatedly, when supplier selection is completed in a vacuum, there are meaningful risks that the criteria will be—at best—parochial and sub-optimized for the company as a whole. In rare cases (although not rare enough) the decision to choose a supplier can be based solely on personal desires/agendas:

"When sourcing goes sour." We were asked to come in because the CEO of ReelSound Systems recognized that they had poor sourcing controls in place. Our assessment revealed that the sourcing manager was routinely "delivering" payments to suppliers personally and, upon further investigation, had been taking kickbacks. This led to painful consequences and the termination of the sourcing manager as well as the supplier (who, as it turns out, had won the business to satisfy their own ulterior motives). After a protracted legal wrangle—nothing short of an ugly mess—the final good news was that by addressing this situation, the company was now able to:

- Have control over the integrity of the sourcing relationship
- Reduce the price for items paid
- Lower inventory levels
- Increase order fulfillment

I'm sad to say this isn't the only situation we've encountered where unethical or illegal activity was taking place under the radar. First let me say that the vast majority of people are ethical, honest, and want to do a good job. If you hire carefully and take care of your people, that's a good default to go by. To protect from malalignment, you need efficient systems and accountability measures to bring those situations out from under the radar and deal with them immediately—or more importantly, to prevent them from ever happening at all.

> **It is weakness and shallow thought that leads to a company relying solely on employee integrity to avoid illegal or dangerous activity!**

As a leader, it is within your power to put controls and processes in place that encourage the selection of suppliers based on the TOTAL COST to the company and its customers—and will also eliminate the potential for irregular activity.

2. At what level are you negotiating your volumes?

When you purchase on the spot market, you're making a simple transaction with a supplier for that specific need. The impact of your total volume or spend over a longer time frame is not considered.

> **When you negotiate with a supplier you are asking them to invest in you as a customer.**

That investment may come in the form of:

- Discounts

- Annual volume rebates

- Resources to support the development of new products

- Commitments to prioritize the company in times of scarcity

- Systems to make releases and daily transactions effortless and seamless

- Payment terms

- Co-branding, and countless other vehicles to add value to the supply chain

- Inventory programs

Of course, the supplier has to evaluate these investments based on the return provided to them. The total volumes, time frame, and commitment will enter into their calculation.

One objection we commonly hear is: "We don't know our volumes in the future so we can't commit to volumes we do not know." Be still, young padawan (a young Jedi for those who are not Star Wars fans), this is a false dichotomy—there are good options! One that we turn to often is making a "commitment of supply" versus a static commitment. A commitment of supply offers the supplier a percentage of your future needs as opposed to a specific quantity. For a primary supplier, for example, you might offer 80 percent of your serviceable needs, assuming they continue to meet quality and service level expectations. For a deeper dive into this valuable intel, read my book, *Implementing Supplier Partnerships*.

3. Have your purchased goods and services been competitively bid in the last three to five years? Reliance on spot markets, short-term agreements and the standard terms printed on purchase orders signal transactional supplier relationships. You also want to (perhaps counterintuitively) regularly look at evergreen (ongoing) contracts. These can feel like "partnerships," but the contracts may not be leveraging the volumes and spend to their full advantage.

4. Do you measure supplier performance? In a tightly run plant, suppliers have to deliver *exactly what is needed when it is needed*—there's no room for inspections, late deliveries, inaccurate picks or defects if you want high performance. Monitoring supplier activity helps you identify any patterns or consistent errors that are slowing down operations—or opportunities for better, money-saving efficiencies.

5. Do you control the release of inbound raw materials? Value-added sourcing agreements can provide for inventory programs like:

- Consignment inventory

- Smaller minimum order quantities

- Block scheduling

You might be able to reduce variable costs by allowing your supplier to manage your inventory. Consider the impact to the buyer and the supplier when you share information and trust the relationship:

- **Benefits to the purchasing company:** Ordering is simplified. *Send me what I need, instead of me submitting an order every time.* The supplier will manage their inventory accordingly, so you stand to reduce your own inventory from this enhanced efficiency. You avoid having to shut down a line due to lack of parts. The result? Time and cost savings!

- You provide your forecast and production schedules to the supplier, choosing if you want some materials all at once, others monthly, etc. In your agreement you stipulate how you want to schedule out your materials and possible payment plan.

- **Benefits for the supplier:** The supplier can use the buyer's information to level load their plant, plan production, and improve their own purchasing, which will in turn benefit the entire process. They can do their own forecasting because they have this standing order over the period of the agreement. Compare this to a company that doesn't know what, when—or if—the next order will be.

All this because you went beyond negotiating just price and quality. The benefits to both parties are off the charts!

6. Are there inbound freight costs buried in your product costs? A common answer we receive to our question, "Who pays the freight on your incoming shipments?" is: "Oh ... well, freight is free." *(Instant eye roll ... never true!)* When we find freight buried in the material cost we see a sign that sourcing is often not strategically managed.

Most suppliers build profit into their freight charges; unbundling freight costs can lead to significant improvements for you. In negotiating a supplier contract, consider how and where the freight cost is included in the price of the product, and discuss with your supplier practical ways to minimize those costs.

7. Has the company conducted a value engineering exercise? As we know, Lean manufacturing and process re-engineering can dramatically improve cycle times and lead times, and lower the costs to process paperwork, products, and services. The same mindset can be applied to the product design itself—and your supplier can become a valuable player in your success!

Design for manufacturing, value engineering, or similar methodologies can dramatically improve the landed cost for an item, explained best in this example:

> **We worked with Maytag Corporation's engineering team to review** the design of a dishwasher. We included our suppliers in the process and together found that we could eliminate a few dozen components. The result was an updated design that reduced the number of raw materials, simplified and sped up the manufacturing process. One specific project led to the elimination of 39 components and dozens of assembly steps!

8. Are you doing documented make-versus-buy analyses? There can be a substantial benefit from making something you typically buy or buying something you typically make. In some cases, you have the scale to justify expanding your fixed-cost base, and at other times the suppliers may offer a cost structure that beats your own. The only way a company will know is if they document their make-versus-buy decisions.

We see cases where a company gets in the habit of doing something one way without analyzing if it is ultimately good for the company. Case in point:

"Tis the season-al." Seasonal Sensations Company manufactures and distributes their own branded products. They built a tremendous brand and loyal customer base. They also realized that their plant sits idle for part of the year due to the seasonal nature of their products. We helped them complete a make-versus-buy analysis which compared contract manufacturers and third-party distribution to their internal cost structure.

The analysis and eventual results showed that if they made the move to outsource, the company's EBITDA would go up 40 percent, and their return on capital would grow more than fourfold!

In this case, the analysis resulted in their making a huge shift in their business model. Many other make-versus-buy decisions may just have you outsource a cost, step, or process to the party best able to take care of it.

Look for these signs and do the math. It will help your company focus on core competencies, grow the company, and earn a better return on your capital. This is what I did ...

You could say I "wrote the book" on negotiating supplier contracts when I published *Implementing Supplier Partnerships*. However, for my own company I outsourced all of our sourcing work to another firm, even though I consider myself an expert at it. Crazy? Nope! It's their specialty. All they do is negotiate contracts on behalf of clients. They have software for it, their people are well trained in it, they have excellent comp structures and get paid out of savings—things that would be difficult for our company to do. And it frees up time for the rest of us to devote toward doing what we do best.

So, do your supplier sourcing homework and uncover some Texas Tea!

#2 SUPPLY CHAIN DESIGN:
Distribution, office, and manufacturing

> **"Space abhors a vacuum." Aristotle may have thought he was only talking about nature.**

A missed Black Gold prospecting opportunity may be found in your supply chain design, specifically, your location(s) of production, distribution and support facilities.

Are you revisiting your footprint/distribution network design? Companies often have more facilities or space than they need to serve their customers. Warehouses may be included in an acquisition deal, customers can require a facility to be maintained to support their operations, company managers might be comfortable operating on a large investment in inventory (remember, you can't sell from an empty cart!) Multiple scenarios like these will eventually end up with a footprint no one would have ever designed from scratch!

And it may be leaking profits.

Most companies are not proactively rethinking their growth in this way until they're literally confronted with a good reason to deal with their particular brand of sprawl. I say, it's better to do it early than wait until it's too late.

The analysis doesn't have to be complicated. A quick-and-dirty sketch of the current distribution network will show you any duplicate locations and will provide the motivation for additional investigation. Here's a scenario to consider:

Every time you add a warehouse, you add inventory because you have to have inventory in every warehouse for it to work. Let's say the plant is located in Chicago and you ship everything to your customers from there. You begin acquiring a bunch of customers in California, so you're considering adding a distribution center there.

Your analysis is to figure out what the lowest total cost would be as a result of this change, so you can decide whether or not it is wise to lease that California warehouse. Compare the costs of shipping your item from Chicago to the customer in Oakland or San Diego, with the costs of sending a truckload of inventory to the California warehouse to be distributed locally from there.

The good news is that this is simply a matter of math. The bad news is that many of us avoid math! Do the math.

Every situation is different in terms of the nature of your customer needs, shipping options and managing the inventory between facilities. The point is to do the analysis, not act from "gut feel" or resignation that it's okay "as it is."

For extra credit, when you do review your footprint and facility network, evaluate the space requirements and locations based on how you should be running the facilities—not simply how you run things today.

During the 2020 pandemic, a client that manufactures and distributes electronic components asked us to help design their future manufacturing and warehouse space. They had been growing and believed they needed a bigger facility to handle their growth. At the end of the first week, we scheduled a sit-down with the leadership team and asked how committed they were to moving—for two reasons: First, we found that over 40 percent of the inventory they kept onsite exceeded what they would use in six months. A little housecleaning would clear up significant space, and good materials planning would keep it sparkling. The second reason was related to manufacturing: We discovered that each project was active on the shop floor for six weeks, and that four and a half of those weeks were wasted. Implementing some Lean manufacturing techniques would increase velocity (Chapter Three). The client did not sign the lease for a new warehouse ... the extra space was no longer needed.

Not only were savings found but ... can you imagine signing a long-term lease a month before the pandemic? Bullet dodged!

Get your markers out. Try a few of the following to see what you learn, or what patterns you recognize in your company:

- *Create a heat map of deliveries* by region, state, or city. Add in your manufacturing and distribution points. (A heat map simply means that you shade in each location based on how much demand you receive from that area).

- *Summarize your biggest shipping lanes* and look for waste, which might include re-shipping inventory between your own facilities, shipping to a customer from a distant warehouse and shipments that come back from where you shipped them.

- *Map clusters of locations that could satisfy demand* for a larger region. This often happens when locations are added through acquisitions or due to a prior customer-specific request.

This is simple to do and provides a springboard from which you and your team can talk about what makes sense for your company. In a situation when the stakes are higher, you'll find more advanced tools to optimize your footprint which will be relevant and worth the effort.

In the prior chapter we reviewed the financial impact of increasing velocity. One reason it is so dramatic is that we find a way to harvest more fruit with existing resources. In assessing supply chain design, remember Aristotle: *Are we truly using our space to fill demand or has available space been a convenient way to avoid solving a real problem?*

#3 SUPPLY PLANNING:
Supply chain management

Sales and Operations Planning (S&OP) refers to the processes the company uses to plan (or forecast) demand, to match up the supply produced to meet that demand, to plan the working capital needed to support production, and integrating those components as a team.

We leverage S&OP in order to:

- Balance supply and demand

- Optimize inventory levels

- Improve customer service

- Enhance decision making and strategic planning

Let's welcome back our Fishy friends. After we addressed the plant changes and the company was producing enough fish to fill their clients' shelves, we ran into another problem. The plant had sped up so much that they started running out of fish, the warehouses ran out of space, and the freight carriers fell behind. If takt time helps you determine the right speed to run a line, S&OP helps you to match sales, supply planning, distribution, finance, and other support departments as well. So, we then embarked on a whole new improvement cycle focused on collaborating throughout the company to synchronize all departments and efforts to serve their customers.

The following are the four main indicators of S&OP that may demand your attention:

1. Are your service levels low? If a company does not have an industry-leading perfect order level, has longer lead times than competitors, or high expediting scrap/warranty costs, then there is likely a significant opportunity to improve planning and S&OP, operations, and EBITDA.

2. Do you measure forecasting; if so, are you doing it adequately and accurately? Companies that do not have the discipline to forecast will put unnecessary burdens on operations. These burdens lead to excess and obsolete (E&O) inventory, overtime, downtime, expediting costs, and—frankly—chaos! If forecast accuracy is low or not measured, it's an indicator that your company is not managing this area effectively and stands to leak profits badly.

This may seem funny from a distance, but another sign that planning is anemic is when the CFO predicts on the 25th of the month that they will hit the budget for the month and then proceeds to fall short—or exceed it—a few days later.

3. Expediting. You may recognize that expediting (the act of taking action to make sure a specific order or event happens on time), has come up throughout this book. It is a clear sign of waste, poor processes, or other obstacles that get in the way— showing up in the following ways:

- *Do we have anyone in the company with "expediting" in their title or job description?*

- *Do we pay meaningful amounts for premium freight or service levels from our suppliers?*

- *Do we see high levels of stress or a blame culture?*

4. Is inventory growing faster than sales? If so, this is a critical indicator of misalignment between production output and market demand. It suggests that forecasting, production planning, and procurement processes are not well synchronized with actual customer needs. This imbalance can lead to excess stock, higher holding costs, and increased risks of obsolescence, all of which tie up capital unnecessarily.

#4 LOGISTICS AND WAREHOUSE MANAGEMENT:
Moving goods and services

Every day we're shipping products from suppliers, between locations, within our facilities, and to customers. Things we do every day add up and can have a significant impact on our costs and our lead times. Even small improvements will create competitive advantages and impact your market position. Let's look at logistics related to moving products between facilities (outside the four walls) and in your warehouses and distribution centers (inside the four walls).

Outside the four walls:

Landed cost. As our economy continues to become more global, the logistics get more complex. Especially in global sourcing, it's helpful to recognize that the cost quoted by a supplier is not a monolithic "product cost." The cost of the actual product is only one of many components and can become a relatively minor one at that. For example, as you compare different suppliers in different regions, you need to consider the following additional costs:

- Value added taxes (VAT), customs and tariffs

- Currency exchange rates and transaction fees

- Shipping (including from the supplier to the port, over the water, and drayage to your facility)

- The working capital required due to longer lead times, and the related impact on flexibility. One major example is the impact on minimum order quantities—smaller shipments add fees and expensive freight premiums.

- The cost of managing a remote supplier. This can require expensive trips, expats, or third-party agents.

The question to consider is whether you have clarity on each of these costs and the total landed cost. The impact of sub-optimizing sourcing decisions in a global network is often dramatic!

Mode selection and capacity utilization. Companies can ship products via small-package vehicles, less-than-truckload (LTL), full truckload, intermodal, rail, ocean, and air. As you can imagine (and probably have experienced) the costs and lead times for each of these vary greatly. Experienced logisticians with good data and software tools will exploit ways to consolidate shipments, zone skip, and move from an expensive to less expensive mode.

We often see a 30 percent reduction in cost as we move between shipping modes (rail is cheaper than intermodal, intermodal is cheaper than over-the-road trucks, full truck loads are cheaper than partial, and partial trucks are cheaper than small package).

"To pay or not to pay." We completed a review of one week's worth of shipments at All Parts Emporium. They primarily shipped less-than-truckload shipments and their shipping department worked hard to negotiate good rates, so they believed they were pretty efficient. However, they didn't actively review upcoming orders to identify opportunities to combine shipments. In our one week of review, we found a number of examples of shipments that literally could have been shipped for free if they had been connected to other loads!

Evaluating opportunities to improve logistics costs and mode optimization tend to require more open-ended questions than other areas. You might ask the following of your operations team to test the waters as to what you'll want to investigate:

- *Could you walk me through how we consolidate loads?*

- *How do we monitor premium freight (air versus ocean, overnight versus standard, over the road versus rail)?*

- *When do you ship small package versus LTL?*

Private fleets. As you consider the cost of moving inventory between you, your suppliers, and your customers, you might also look at the utilization of any company-owned or leased assets you might have. Private fleets are rapidly becoming less relevant as specialized third-party providers (3PLs) continue to develop their tools, systems, and infrastructure. Think of this as a make-versus-buy decision which we covered in the prior section.

If your company has a fleet of some kind, look into how it is measured and monitored. Here's an example that flew under this client's radar for years:

"Too much track ... not enough tracking." We conducted a diagnostic review for a large commodity manufacturing and distribution client, with a fleet of hundreds of rail cars and contracts with many railroads. We reviewed and benchmarked the rail contracts and rates and saw that their reports showed a 100-percent utilization rate. Naturally, our spidey sense started to tingle, telling us this was too good to be true! So, we talked to the manager, Luis, and asked how the utilization rate was calculated.

We anticipated that they tracked loaded ton miles versus a standard, or something similar. Instead, Luis told us they track whether each rail car was used in a month. They had 213 rail cars, and they had 213 loads in the month, so this would show that their utilization was 100 percent—every rail car was used in the month, so this was viewed as a win. There was some logic to this. However, we calculated that each rail car had a practical capacity to travel 500 miles in a day or over 11,000 miles in a month. When you consider loading and unloading times, you might set your target utilization for a rail car at 60 percent of potential miles in a month. With this in mind, the calculation of 100 percent used the wrong denominator to be helpful. When we calculated the miles each rail car *actually* traveled in a month with product, they fell to less than 10 percent capacity!

This discovery opened up a process review and process improvements which allowed the company to *reduce their fleet by 70 percent*—without diminishing customer service levels! The excess rail cars were the result of a loose process and a lack of thoughtful oversight. The new, improved process now prevented the company from incurring non-value-adding expenses.

Non-value-added shipments. Customers value freight costs that get good product to them. Sometimes you gain an advantage by providing that shipment for "free," and sometimes they pay the freight separately. They will not, however, pay for freight to, say, move materials or inventory between your locations. Be sure to look at all freight and logistics costs between company locations. These costs should be viewed as an exception and managed like scrap, downtime or unutilized labor.

Inside the four walls:

Inventory control. Banks tend to require full physical inventories to be taken when the company demonstrates that their perpetual inventory is not, or may not, be accurate. (By "perpetual inventory" we mean that the company knows the balance by tracking so they can calculate their current balance.) If they have solid inventory controls in place and conduct cycle counts, then the bank will rely on the perpetual inventory. If the bank is not comfortable with that, then we look closely at how well they record inventory transactions, how well they use their system, and how they physically control the materials.

Material Resource Planning (MRP) systems only work if your bills of material (BOMs) and your perpetual inventory are accurate. If either is wrong the system will suggest purchases and inventory moves that are INCORRECT. This will lead to increases in inventory and space requirements, which in turn will lead to lower order fulfillment rates. In the words of *Ghostbusters'* Dr. Vinkman, "This would be bad." Important tip!

The short story is, if you do not know what you have in inventory, you will inevitably hold more than you need. When this happens, the extra working capital required is the tip of the iceberg of the company's problems! You may have noticed in Chapter One that we mentioned inventory in a handful of the signs showing a company relies on workarounds. Our bodies cannot be healthy without a good diet; in a similar way our companies cannot be efficient without good inventory control.

Labor management. The velocity and efficiency concepts we discussed in Chapter Three apply to managing a warehouse as well, in the areas of receiving, put-away, material handling, and picking orders.

At ProAction, we start with these questions to understand how effectively labor is managed in a distribution operation.

1. *Do you track order picking rates and times? If so, do you use them to predict the hours required to pick the day's orders?*

2. *Is labor utilization calculated?* No question, efficiency is a good thing to measure! It shows how well you complete your required tasks to fill orders. However, it may not tell the whole story. ***Calculating labor utilization means you compare the total time predicted to pick all orders versus what you paid in total payroll.***

The Black Gold revealed is how much of your payroll is going towards non-value-adding tasks or items.

3. *How are you handling seasonality?* Many distribution operations have dramatic fluctuations in volume. We often look at the variation in picks-per-labor-hour throughout the year.

4. *Are pickers picking multiple or single orders at any one time?*

5. *How often do pickers have to look for an item?*

6. *Do you see any congestion?* Do pickers have to wait or navigate clogged aisles?

It is common to find that pickers are picking a fraction of what they could accomplish. The system, layout, picklist order, and the way products are organized all combine to make it difficult to pick. These six questions will show you where there is an improvement opportunity. We have seen companies increase the orders picked by 50 percent to over 100 percent while making life easier for the workers!

The slots! Physical layout. The setup of a warehouse will impact the speed and efficiency related to receiving and picking. An often-overlooked way to think about the layout is the slotting strategy—the approach you use to decide where to put different products you store. Here are two specific questions to consider, either of which may uncover meaningful opportunities to improve:

- *When you ask about the "slotting strategy," do you get a blank stare or an answer that does not consider the frequency that the part or component is consumed or shipped to a customer?*

- *When was the last time the slotting strategy was updated? Demand patterns change; do you change with them?*

"Playing the slots." We visited the warehouse of Sharkfin Pool Supply. We asked Reggie, the manager, how he decided where to put each item they stored. "By weight," he replied, "We put the heavier products in the back because it makes it easier to use a forklift or pallet jack to put them away." This made good sense based on that aspect of material handling, but not for picking.

A good slotting strategy always starts with the frequency with which a part is picked, because you want to reduce the distance traveled to put together the average order. You can then balance minimizing that time with avoiding traffic jams.

As we worked with them on the warehouse layout, we noticed another improvement waiting to be made: They had not updated their slotting strategy in years. With new product additions and changing order patterns, pickers had to travel longer distances and would run into "traffic". It took longer than necessary to pick orders!

In two days, we literally doubled the orders they could pick by combining all single-part orders into one pick list. This meant that one picker could make a trip through the warehouse and fill 30–40 orders at a time. The client was now able to cut their order lead times from four to seven days, down to 24 hours—with their current workforce!

Big picture upside

In Chapter Three we explored how accelerating the pace of filling customer demand can drive many outsized returns. The side benefit is that pursuing velocity naturally positions the company to leverage processes and tools that de-risk the company and make it easier to lead.

Think of this chapter as the other side of the coin. We applied the same concept to distribution centers and the facility footprint as a whole. Identifying these opportunities often requires time and attention. The data already exists and simply needs to be organized and reviewed!

Take a breath and carve out some time to ask the questions. The oil may be just below the surface and will be there when you're ready to tap it!

Supply chain and sourcing: Bottom line

➡ Learning to wield your suppliers' capacity and their supply chain reveals hidden value that will set you apart. Negotiate great partnership agreements with the best suppliers so they're investing in YOU.

➡ In addition to quality, monitor your sourcing in relation to inventory, design efficiencies, freight fees, and shipping charges, make versus buy.

➡ "Black Gold" opportunities can be found in your supply chain design (location(s) of production, distribution and support facilities). Measure forecasting to relieve the pressure on operations.

CHAPTER FIVE

Keeping Score—How to Define What Success Looks Like

"If you tell me how I will be measured,
I will know how to work the system."
—Perry Hall

IF YOU'RE A FOOTBALL FAN like I am (lifetime Chicago Bears—don't judge me 😊), you have probably noticed how the last two minutes of a game always seems to translate to 15 minutes! After that two-minute warning, coaches closely manage every single second based on the score, the yard line, if they're trailing (making every second count) or winning (shaving seconds off the clock), and how much time is left.

Can you imagine a football game in which the team was not allowed to look at the clock, the scoreboard, or the yard line? Close your eyes and picture how wrong that would be!

Worse yet, what if the players and coaches were given different data to manage the game, such as fan reactions, frustration level of the referees, or beer sales? Can you imagine the iconic Chicago Bear's football coach Mike Ditka at the end of a game, having to use those measures instead of the scoreboard? He would have probably popped a vein!

Yet, this is exactly what we often ask of our workers and managers every day.

For any company that wants to meet a goal with any semblance of success (and be profitable at it), two things are needed: *clarity and predictability.*

Measuring the value levers of hidden risk and opportunity brings clarity through metrics, analysis, and observation. Lacking these measures or not paying attention to them can cost a company dearly.

> **What is worse than having a blind spot? Believing something's true when it isn't!**

The wrong metrics or inaccurate analysis can do even more harm because they will lead us confidently—down the wrong path, in the wrong direction.

We're going to explore methods of keeping score, what does NOT work, and how to tell if the "star to every wandering bark"[8] is true north or throwing us out of the virtuous cycle known as continuous improvement! We will focus on three key concepts:

1. **Metrics**

2. **Cost Accounting (Accuracy)**

3. **The Closed-Loop System**

Together, these keys will enable you to prioritize and accurately assess whether or not you're solidly on the exciting path toward achieving your vision.

> **Defining what success looks like gives life to your North Star.**

#1: Metrics

When we're tasked by a prospective or current business owner to conduct due diligence on a company, we start with a focus on how they measure success. Too often, we find:

- A lack of metrics

- Leaders are not paying attention to the metrics they're using

- The wrong metrics, or combination of metrics, have become the standard

- Management is not measuring variation, or deviations in things like safety, scrap, customer service levels, quality, cycle times, warranty costs, or employee engagement

> **When variation in your metrics is reduced, costs and stress are reduced.**

Let's dive in...

If we do not have clear goals and know what success looks like, we meander. This is human nature—yet it doesn't work so well in business. The axiom goes: *If you can't measure it, you can't manage it!* If you don't measure throughput, you cannot predict what you're going to accomplish in a day. If you have not hit your numbers, you won't know why. If you don't measure your processes, you won't know how efficiently, or inefficiently, your line is running.

It should work like this: Every day each line, team, or worker knows what they need to accomplish to satisfy customer demand. At the end of each day, they review how they performed to the plan. When there is a gap, there is an issue with the plan or execution. The appropriate metrics provide clear guidelines to help everyone in the company literally land on, and stay on, the same page.

Think about it like a checkbook or personal accounting app. Have you ever noticed how, if you don't plan out your spending for the month and track it, *you always spend more than you had budgeted for*? (I think this might be Newton's 4th law of physics ...)

Clearly, we want metrics, and we want the right ones.

> **Make sure you are measuring against what you actually want to accomplish—that which is best for your customers, your employees, and your company.**

For more wisdom on how metrics can help or hinder operations, I turn to my good friend and colleague at ProAction, Perry Hall[9]. Not only is Perry always the life of the party, he's our guru on Lean manufacturing, having learned it in Japan at the knee of the masters at Toyota. He has the amazing ability to walk through a plant and be back in an hour knowing exactly what to do—and how to relay it to the client with empathy and humor. Lots of humor.

Perry often says: *"If you tell me how I will be measured, I will know how to 'work' the system"*—an interesting thing about human nature. For example, if a company measures how many units are produced in an hour, then the workers will make decisions to match that measure. However, strong hourly production does NOT mean customer demand is being served. ***It is too easy to design metrics to look good without doing good.*** Sometimes well-intentioned metrics drive unintended poor performance ...

"It's a wrap!" We were called in to conduct an assessment of George's company, Mighty Tasty Meals, which manufactures ready-to-eat sandwiches. As an employee incentive George set up their pay based on piecework, how many wraps they could produce in an hour. Easy to understand why George would go this route—the workers would be motivated to produce more sandwiches!

The assembly process had ingredients that came down the line and workers added them to make the meal pack and wrapped it up. The line workers had been setting the speed of the conveyor slightly faster than they could handle, with the idea of increasing efficiency. However, in short order we found that this was bad for business.

Why? Because George was measuring success using the wrong metric, and in isolation. Speeding up the line made the process sloppier because more food fell off at the end of the line and was subsequently tossed out as scrap. The company had never measured or tracked ingredient scrap—they just purchased more inventory.

Now they had a huge waste problem they didn't know about— they'd been throwing away at least 10 percent of materials! It turned out that, while profitable, George's company was *losing millions* in ingredients per year. To boot, because of the way they'd measured incentives for their employees, they essentially were paying bonuses for this undesired outcome!

They were measuring the wrong thing and not measuring the important things. These were the actions we recommended:

- Start tracking scrap (it costs real money!)

- Schedule and organize production to meet customer demand.
- Measure and reward workers for hitting the schedule on time and with no waste.

We set up a system of schedule attainment, and if the worker hit the schedule, they got full pay plus bonus. The goal was to complete what had been planned for the day, based on the best system possible for workers to achieve goals—while ensuring quality for the customer, maintaining efficiencies for the company and rewarding excellent work.

Let's springboard from this story to outline six healthy practices to keep score effectively:

1. Metrics are tied to the company vision, goals, and performance. When you have a clear vision and solid understanding of the financials, you can design metrics that link behavior directly to what matters. A good way to view this is to start with the metrics at the highest level, then cascade them down to each division, function, department, line, and team. Each metric should align back with the basic vision and goal for the company!

2. Everyone has a number. Everybody should know what their goal is. Every single person in the company knows what success looks like for them, personally, because it's measured.

3. Metrics cover the key topics. For operations it would normally include:

- *Safety. How safe are your employees and your assets? How often do safety exceptions occur?*

- **Quality.** *Do your services and products achieve their design? Does it happen on the first try? What is poor quality costing you?*

- **Cost.** *How well are you satisfying customer demand in line with your designed cost structure?*

- **Delivery.** *How often do you provide your service when promised or requested?*

- **Morale.** *How engaged are your employees? Are they staying or escaping?*

- **Sustainability.** *How prepared is your company to thrive even if your leadership team disengages from the company? And how well does your company steward its resources?*

4. Leading and lagging indicators are reviewed. Regarding safety, for example, we have a lagging indicator that shows it has been a number of days since the last incident in which someone was hurt. A leading indicator could include, for example in the case of monitoring company vehicles, how often your drivers exceed the speed limit. While, assuredly, there are dozens to consider, here are a few leading indicators we often find lacking and impactful:

- **Overall Equipment Effectiveness (OEE).** This term applies specifically to manufacturing settings, but the concept may be applied in any business that satisfies demand. Compare actual production to your theoretical limit. In a plant, this is defined by multiplying your *first-pass yield* (how often your product/service goes through the process without defect on the first try), *designed/optimal line speed* (how fast the line or process should run) and *uptime* (how much of the time your line or operation was running). Note, even world-class companies that focus immense resources to measure this will achieve 85 percent. Don't worry about where you are, focus on where you can go!

- **Schedule attainment**. This has become one of my favorite metrics, requiring three steps:

  Step 1: Predict what the operation will produce in a specific time period.

  Step 2: Track actual production during that time period, noting any exceptions or issues that come up.

  Step 3: Compare them.

  Schedule attainment recognizes that a company develops a schedule or plan and then executes. Measuring schedule attainment allows you to evaluate both how well you schedule and how well you execute!

  One of the first questions we ask a plant manager during a tour is, "How are things going?" If they respond, "Great, all the machines are running," or "our efficiencies are well over 100 percent," then we know they're likely scheduling the plant based on a "push" methodology—meaning you build schedules to minimize changeovers and downtime, pushing work through the system according to a schedule. In contrast, the "pull" methodology measures schedule attainment to fill customer orders based on real-time demand or consumption, which promotes responsive production. A pull system tends to focus your operation on serving the customer, while push systems pursue efficiency. Serving customers is an actionable pursuit!

- **Employee engagement.** Employees can be divided into three groups: actively engaged, passively engaged and actively disengaged. Have you been on a church or charity committee and noticed that one or two people do 80 percent of the work? These people are actively engaged. Their production is dramatically higher than those who simply show up and those who actually resent the organization. Track that variation. See the Go Deeper Appendix for more on how to monitor employee engagement.

- **Production per labor hour.** This is simple to calculate: Take your sales or production each period (normally weekly or monthly) and divide it by the number of labor hours that produced the output. The point of measuring this is to look at trends over time. We often find that companies demonstrate very high levels during parts of the year and low in others, offering opportunities to leverage efficiencies.

5. Measures are visible. I feel that a potential Yogi Berra quote would work here: *Visible metrics are more likely to be seen!* Every department should have their performance indicators on display—they drive behavior.

6. Metrics become a conversation starter. As soon as we introduce the idea of metrics, people often become concerned that they or their work will be judged. It is a valid worry!! ***Metrics are not conclusions—they start conversations.*** If metrics are used as a cudgel, they will serve to demoralize the team and encourage people to find ways to circumvent the system—circling back to Perry's observation.

Here is another cautionary tale with this moral: Be careful what you ask for. You will get it!

"Thinking Outside the Box." Boxtop Cardboard Company bought large, standard-sized pressed board from their supplier, cut it to the right size, and then made boxes. Lots of impressive equipment, but a simple process. In a financial statement review, they noticed a high amount of scrap. Since leadership was developing a continuous improvement culture, they decided to challenge their team: If they could reduce the cost of scrap, they would receive a bonus!

The team dug in and studied the issue. They found that most of the scrap came from the extra material they cut off from the standard pressed boards they received. So, they started ordering custom-width boards to match their orders. The cost of custom-width boards was higher than the standard-width size. On top of this, they were now ordering dozens of differently-sized boards for different uses, thus having to maintain more inventory.

As a result of these changes, the company committed more working capital to buy the inventory, taking up additional warehouse space, and they paid more for the custom materials. It was more expensive and required more cash! Unintended consequences ...

The cherry on the icing on the cake, the double whammy—they paid bonuses to the team for taking action on this initiative. Ouch.

#2: Cost accounting (accuracy)

This client's story is the best explanation of accuracy in cost accounting ...

"Ice that Idea!" Frostytime Company manufactures and distributes ice-melter products. They were quite profitable, with stable clients and a fairly simple supply chain. But the business was highly seasonal, such that they shipped most of their product in the autumn season. They decided to add a fertilizer product line that would use the same equipment and sell into the same retail chains as their ice-melter lines. A thoughtful plan!

As we started our engagement, Mila, the CEO, told us the fertilizer business was significantly more profitable than their ice-melter business. She wanted to look for ways to increase their fertilizer business and maybe lean away from their ice-melter offering.

As our team dug in, we realized they were allocating all of their warehouse, distribution and overhead costs *across ice melter and fertilizer equally.* Therefore, we noticed some differences between the two products:

- Ice melter was sold in pallets of 50lb. bags. Fertilizer was often sold by eight-ounce bottles or by the case, with partial pallets.
- Ice melter was sold as one simple heavy-duty bag. Fertilizer was packaged to attract retail customers—bright colors, multiple sizes, thus requiring more expensive packaging.

- Ice melter was easy to package and required little labor. The fertilizer product had multiple packaging sizes and required special machines and additional labor to fill them.

When we reallocated the equipment, overhead, and distribution costs, it became clear that the company had it exactly backwards! They had a simple ice-melter business that was literally printing money, and they had a high-needs fertilizer business that was modestly profitable.

It is worth it to dig in and make sure that your cost assumptions are roughly right, not precisely wrong!

Good cost-accounting systems do the following:

- *Allocate or spread overhead* based on thoughtful, activity-based methods.

- *Review and update standards annually.* This means that each year you will review the extent to which your approach to assigning costs to each product/service aligns with reality. The annual approach allows you to see patterns over multiple runs and to avoid using stale numbers that haven't been reviewed in years.

- *Collaborate cross-functionally.* When you roll standards or evaluate product costs, assemble a team that includes finance, sales, and operations. This will ensure that the approach is vetted by the full team, and each department will have a better understanding of their real cost structure.

- *Conduct audits.* Set aside time and budget to have internal or external experts test and evaluate your cost accounting and overhead allocations.

Extra Credit Action: The points above describe a good traditional cost-accounting system. Investigate Lean Cost Accounting to go next level! In short, lean accounting enables a company to support good decision making, to reduce waste, and to improve cash flow[10].

#3: The closed-loop system

If you want to ensure solid metrics and accurate cost accounting, your best bet is to use the closed-loop system. Generally speaking, this system means that you:

1. Predict what you expect or plan to happen in a period of time for a quote, a project, etc. What will happen next quarter, this month, and today?

2. Use visible metrics to track progress.

3. Review progress throughout the time period.

4. Implement containment steps to keep on track.

5. After the period is complete, use that information to drive problem solving and corrective action.

> *"We need to realize that our path to transformation is through our mistakes. We're meant to make mistakes, recognize them, and move on to become unlimited."*
> —Attributed to Yehuda Berg[11]

Here is an example of the closed-loop system applied to a quoting process:

Metallica Inc. provided metal coating for parts supplied by the customer. Every order was different based on the shape and size of the part, the specific coating required, the setup time required and the number of pieces they would run. While every order was custom, they did share common traits that made it easier to quote new customers over time. Their quoting system worked like this:

1. *Quote.* We quote a new part and win the business.
2. *Setup.* We set up our bills of material and our standards for the number of people and time required to coat the items.
3. *Produce.* As we run an actual order, we collect the data on materials used, line time required, and labor hours. While the order is running, supervisors monitor performance and jump in with countermeasures to help the team succeed in hitting their numbers and/or schedule on a daily basis.
4. *Postproduction Review.* After the job is complete, we compare the actual performance against the standards and the quote. *If our actual production did not match the predicted cost or timing, was it an execution issue or misquoted?* For any gaps or discrepancies, we dig in to understand if it is an operational issue or a quoting issue.

This information was used to drive problem solving and continuous improvement.

It is easy for a company to leave out a step or two from this habit. However, think about the impact that one misquoted item could have on a company, when all future quotes are based on what they have done before—and they never figured out that it was incorrect!

This is a moment where I say: If you ONLY applied this one idea from the book, you would see A LOT of progress and energy! It inspires me to share this bold statement:

> **If you develop a problem-solving culture based on a healthy closed-loop system, you will see a minimum of 20 percent improvement in velocity and performance.**

Top ten indicators of opportunity

Now that we have talked about what excellence looks like, which indicators will tell you that your company does NOT have clarity and you're making life hard for yourselves?

1. *Metrics are not visible* in each department. It is not obvious what success looks like for the day. When you walk through a work area, can you tell how they're doing, or are you watching a football game with no scoreboard?

2. *Employees are not as productive* as they'd like to be. When asked how they know if they're doing a good job, a worker responds (likely with a twinkle in their eye): "Well if no one is yelling at me, I must be doing pretty well!"

3. *It has been more than 12 months since* standards or overhead allocations were rolled or updated.

4. *The CFO/accountant is not able to provide* a thoughtful explanation for how overhead is allocated.

5. *A cross-functional team has not reviewed* Customer or SKU/Service Income Statements (see Chapter Two!)

6. ***Your company does not maintain a closed-loop metric system***, one in which no one stays stagnant—you either get better or you get worse.

7. ***A project-oriented or job-shop company*** does not measure quote accuracy.

8. ***Schedule attainment is not measured.***

9. ***The CFO and/or CEO do not know*** their experience modifier (E-Mod) rate. Every company pays for workers' compensation insurance tied to their industry. Based on your claims history, you pay above or below the set rates for your industry. An E-Mod rate of .9 means the company pays 90 percent of the industry rates, an E-Mod rate of 1.55 means they pay 155 percent. This rate provides an external benchmark of the relative safety of the company's workforce. Not only is this a critical metric—literally life and death—it also exposes how leadership uses metrics.

10. ***Invoice accuracy/denials/chargebacks are not measured or tracked.*** Credit memos, chargebacks, denied claims, and inaccurate invoices all indicate potential buckets of improvement. If you do not actively track and measure these items, it is unlikely that they're well managed.

To highlight areas where you may have an opportunity to better emulate high-performing companies, ask:

» *Are invoices submitted within 24 hours of service?*
» *Are more than .5 percent of bills or invoices rejected or changed by the customer?*

These indicators will help you assess clarity within a company quickly. If you find an exception in any of these areas, there is oil under that farmland! Start digging!

Big picture upside

I made a bold claim in this chapter: "If you develop a problem-solving culture based on a healthy closed-loop system, you will see a minimum of 20 percent improvement in velocity and performance."

That 20 percent impact is just the beginning. We will explore this more fully in the final chapters, but I'll plant this seed now: ***The real prize here is building a HABIT of curiosity and continuous improvement.*** Put a stake in the ground. Set targets, predict your outcomes. Back to football, monitor that scoreboard during the game and take action. Then watch the game films and adjust! This is how you develop a company that will serve the customer, service each other and function with or without your personal intervention.

How to prepare? ***First, let the past go!*** You're in the "awareness" stage at this point, getting curious and asking questions about how the company is run *today* in order to wake up the organization to hidden risks or opportunities to make life easier and to find Shocking Profit.

Take these steps to develop some tactical wins:

1. Appoint someone on your team to investigate the *Top Ten Indicators of Opportunity* (you can find these in the *Go Deeper Appendix*). The results they find might become a good reason to bring in an expert or study one of the great systems to manage your company, such as Danaher, the Entrepreneur Operating System (EOS) or Toyota.

2. Appoint a team to review the findings and propose one or two metrics or areas to which you can apply a closed-loop system.

3. Show interest. Ask about the metric or new process they have added. Go see it in action. Celebrate any wins that come (and I'm sure they will!)

4. Show *a little more* interest. If you practice tennis for ten minutes a day, every day, you will get much better than playing eight hours in a row just a few times!

5. Model potential improvement areas in your income statement. What would the impact on your profitability be if you reduced the cost of materials or produced 15 percent to 20 percent more product with your existing infrastructure and staff?

6. Give the team time to settle into this new practice or approach. Don't try to make sweeping changes until you have completed Sections II and III of this book!

Defining what success looks like: Bottom line

➡ For any company that wants to meet a goal with any semblance of success (and be profitable at it), two things are needed: clarity and predictability.

➡ Pay attention to your metrics—when variation in your metrics is reduced, costs and stress are reduced. If you can't measure it, you can't manage it!

➡ Good metrics and accurate cost accounting are leveraged in a closed-loop system. If you develop a problem-solving culture based on a healthy closed-loop system, you will see a minimum of 20 percent improvement in velocity and performance.

CHAPTER SIX

Add Value by Reducing Risk— and Quantify it!

"It is not the strongest of the species that survives, nor the most intelligent that survives. It is the one that is most adaptable to change."
—Charles Darwin

WHO COULD FORGET THE 1983 comedy drama, "Risky Business,[12]**"** starring Tom Cruise in his breakout role? Joel is plagued by unforeseen risks as he agrees to a less-than-transparent business plan to run a temporary brothel out of his parent's home—in order to pay for the damage he did to his dad's sports car. Well intentioned plan, though fraught with risk!

Joel may have learned a lesson from his risky behavior. The car in the lake became the least of his problems! In business the risks are often subtle and can even masquerade as harmless or irrelevant "facts of life."

Risk is inherent in business transactions, especially when acquiring another company or a new platform. So, let's look to our PE friends for some clear guidance on how to become aware of potential undisclosed risks, assessing those situations, and seeing how you can take purposeful action to mitigate the risk *plus* find hidden value!

How success hides risk—and opportunity

It is easy to believe that a company with healthy EBITDA,(Earnings Before Interest, Taxes, Depreciation and Amortization) a humming production line and happy employees will promise big financial returns—until it doesn't.

We see situations where clients take an IIWII ("It Is What It Is") attitude as standing operating procedure. They may know their business is exposed to a risk, but they move forward anyway, hoping things will continue to be okay. Or (more likely), they're not even overtly aware of the risk. It is just part of their "normal." For example, when we find a company with a firefighting culture, it's a surefire bet that a steady hum of tension and stress follows. Every order may require manual intervention to fill. Often, it never occurs to anyone that this is an important indicator of "risky business."

Another common situation I see is the fear of uncovering problems that will make the company or brand "look bad," so those issues get swept under the rug.

What's actually happening here?

"The Workaround Risk." *Still Alice*[13] is a movie about a smart, successful, hardworking professor, Alice (played by Julianne Moore). She contracted early onset Alzheimer's. Shockingly, her decline after the diagnosis was quick—within months she was incapable of recognizing her family. How did this happen so fast?

The answer: It didn't. Alice had contracted the disease much earlier, but she had become an adapter. As she started to forget things, she set up systems to help her keep the things she needed, such as car keys, in place. She used her smartphone to remind her of her classes, appointments, and anything else she had to do. She was so smart and driven that she adapted to many of the challenges in the normal course of her life—until she couldn't sustain it any longer.

How does this play out in a company? Remember Joe from Chapter One? He didn't trust the computer to tell him they had a part in stock. So, did he gather the leadership of the company and dig into the root cause of the issue? Of course not! Joe was not in the leadership sphere, and didn't have, nor believe that he had, the authority to do that.

But Joe was determined to do his job right, so he adapted by finding a workaround. He is one of throngs of hard-working, caring people who put out fires all day long. They expedite orders and get the job done. And thank God for them! Because of their hard work the company is successful.

What is also true is that those workaround actions obfuscate the seriousness of the inadequacy of their system. *Their success hides the risk.*

The risks of not seeing the risks

It is one thing to see the signs or believe that a risk exists. It is another to accept that the risk is real and take action to eliminate, manage or mitigate it.

> **When you see a risk, take steps to address it.**

When laid out like this it seems obvious, doesn't it? However, here are the other things we see that often happen instead:

- *Getting angry.* The tendency is to launch an investigation or spend time and energy looking for a culprit. *Who is at fault? Who can we blame?*

- *Avoiding the issue.* Some risks require real change. They may require us to leave old, well-tested approaches behind. This can be painful and scary. It can also feel oddly disloyal to those who set up the current system. We rationalize inaction.

- *Discounting the importance.* This is especially easy if there are no good data or metrics to support the facts.

- *Succumbing to peer pressure.* There are times when a solution to a fundamental problem will be good for the company, but hard on one department or individual. Politics come into play.

- *Getting used to the situation.* As with the example of Alice and Joe, situations rarely pop up and go from non-symptomatic to highly painful overnight. The situation can take years to build and becomes difficult to see with the naked eye.

See if you recognize any of these responses in yourself or your exec team. If so, *resolve to accept the presence of risk in your company—that it is real and deserves appropriate attention.*

Gaining awareness and acceptance of the reality of risk brings good news: You'll be positioning yourself to see the opportunity. To borrow a Gold Rush phrase, "there's oil in them thar hills!" And (thank you, Jed) maybe right under the farm!

> **Position yourself to see the opportunity that risk can reveal.**

Examining these risks is not just an exercise in avoiding pain or thorny situations. Problematic processes and controls that allow risk to fester will eventually cause poor financial performance and hold a company back from growing and scaling.

The punchline: In over twenty-five years of completing operational diligence, we have never killed a deal! We identify risks to create awareness, not to cause panic or worry about falling skies. Every operational risk, especially when identified early, *has a solution.* And if there are risks that don't have a silver bullet, managing exposure is only possible with awareness.

A second punchline, which is why you and I are here together: *Shocking Profit!* When done well, inoculations to risk provide their own ROI. Addressing margin compression, for example, leads to increased margins. Shoring up against business interruption risk will create new stability and increase capacity. Increasing worker safety will help you scale and keep good employees.

Invisible enemies are tough to fight! *Who are these scary monsters in my closet? And why didn't I see them coming?*

My quote in the introduction to Section I bears repeating here: *Unrecognized problems do not get solved! Undiscovered value does not get mined!*

"Walking the Process." A private equity firm found a good company to invest in. Peerless Products, Inc., passed all the financial audits: They were profitable, their customers loved them, and they were growing. They had Ray, an engaged leader who grew up in the business, worked every job in the company, developed strong relationships, and was passionate about his trusted team.

In less than sixty months, the company had grown from $40 million to over $160 million in sales! The investor was planning their exit from the company, selling it to someone who would take them national.

Then Ray began to see that Peerless was hitting its revenue numbers but not profitability. Some numbers just weren't making sense. So, he dug deeper, walking himself through the process—from a customer placing an order, to designing the structure, purchasing the materials and components needed, manufacturing, to shipping and installation in the field.

Doing a detailed walkthrough of every step never seemed relevant in the past. But now that there was a thread loose in the sweater, and Ray pulled it. What he discovered was that as the company grew, many of the processes no longer had the checks and balances he personally oversaw when the company was small. Just two examples of what he found was now happening:

- They would buy extra parts and materials to make about 5% additional structures than the customer ordered, which allowed them to address damaged units and extra orders. They charged the customer for all the inventory purchased for that order. Most of the time, they ended up not needing all the materials they purchased and paid for, so those materials were put into inventory—to sit. This made the company look more profitable on paper than it was in reality. In short, their process recognized expenses as an asset on every job!

- Not only had they thought the job was more profitable than it was, they thought they had a valuable asset in the remaining inventory. Ray realized they lacked controls over sourcing. When a project manager got the material list from engineering, they were free to buy whatever they decided was needed. There was no check in the system that they were ordering according to the design.

- The company had been spending $6 million per year in excess of market prices! Not because of any wrongdoing, but because they didn't have anyone focused on negotiating well with suppliers (as we discussed in Chapter Four). Sourcing was conducted on a job-by-job basis. They weren't leveraging the collective volumes of all their projects over a three-to-five-year period. The company had been doing it this way in order to get their projects shipped every day.

The PE firm was planning for the sale of a company that had tripled in size. It would earn their investors over $100 million. However, because of this new information, they had to delay the sale and pull out all the stops—hire a new CEO, bring in experts like us to revamp and streamline processes, and more—to avoid losing their equity in the company altogether.

This company's story is a sad and perfect example of where an issue or risk escalates to dangerous levels before it is diagnosed, making it difficult to recover and recoup losses.

We can have sympathy for people and companies who suffer the consequences of something they truly didn't know about or recognize. However, intention and ignorance do not protect us from harm. And sometimes the risk doesn't show symptoms until late in the process.

> **With early awareness comes a better chance of planning for, and addressing, risky business.**

The cure tends to be non-invasive, low-cost, and effective. And the secondary (and often overlooked) benefit is that eliminating risk will provide collateral benefit in seemingly unrelated areas!

Eight places to find hidden risk (and mine value)

Here is how we view risk categories:

Business: Risks related to customer concentration, disruptive technologies, competition, market changes, and substitutes. These are risks that often dramatically limit the value of a company.

Financial: Risks related to cash flow, credit, interest rates, fraud, or irregular activities, currencies, shrinkage, unbudgeted capex needs, reduction in the value of an asset, and market fluctuations. A business that is overly reliant on a single customer or supplier can also face significant financial risk if that relationship is disrupted.

Operational: Risks related to the day-to-day operations of the business, such as equipment failures, worker safety, supply chain disruptions, or errors and omissions in products or services. These risks can impact productivity and profitability and may also affect the business's reputation. One common risk is single-sourced suppliers. This can create a disaster if that supplier has a disruption.

Margin compression: Risk in which changes to the costs of inputs, key employee attrition, or scaling will put negative pressure on profitability.

Legal and regulatory: Risks related to compliance with laws and regulations, such as employment laws, health and safety regulations, and environmental regulations. Failure to comply with these can result in fines, lawsuits, or damage to the business's reputation.

Reputational: Risks related to the public perception of the business, such as negative publicity or customer complaints. A damaged reputation can lead to a loss of customers, difficulty attracting new business, and challenges in retaining employees.

Cybersecurity: Risks related to the security of digital information, such as customer data, financial information, and intellectual property. Cyberattacks can result in data breaches, theft of confidential information, and financial losses.

Succession Planning: Risks related to employee attrition. Is the company preparing to fill roles in the company if a key employee is no longer actively employed?

Five questions to help you uncover hidden risk

The one thing we know is that we don't know what is going to come our way. Economic cycles, black swan events, natural disasters, new competitors, evolving customer needs, turnover, inaccurate forecasts—we cannot control any of these events. Worrying about the weather won't bring out the sun! Here is what we do know:

> **We can control our response to risk factors, internal and external. We can control our preparation.**

Knowledge is power! So here are some questions to ask:

1. Does your company rely on tribal knowledge? Tribal knowledge is good. You want your employees to know what to do and where to find it. But it is dangerous to rely on it! On a basic level, companies that rely on employees to know what to do, where to look, what file to use, what tool to use in an operation, how to complete a changeover, how to schedule production, how to quote, or many other tasks, would suffer great loss with even nominal attrition.

Do you have protections from this risk, such as:

- Ensuring the operation is as productive with the boss there or not there, at least for the short term?

- Documenting work instructions and creating an onboarding process that includes more than on-the-job training?

- A robust customer relationship management system which documents all customers, prospects, quotes, agreements, and bids?

- Storage facilities that are bin-located, and cycle counts which demonstrate that items are actually located where the system shows?

If any of the above are missing, it is a sign that you may be relying too much on the knowledge of workers to operate smoothly (review Chapter One!)

2. Do assets on the books not live up to the label? If inventory is shown as an asset on the financials today, there's a good argument (as we see in Ray's case) that it also behaves like a liability! Some inventory is clearly long in the tooth or is not attractive to the market at the price level assigned.

Three common paths for unsellable inventory include:

- **Building excess inventory over time.** In many cases, this happens gradually, building or buying 10–15 percent more each year than needed. Then, a few years later you have a major liability hiding as an asset.

- **Obsolescence.** Regardless of the physical age of the inventory, things like shelf life, disruptive new technologies, or new model years can all lead to an unsellable asset.

- **Commitment to an inventory position for a new product.** For many companies that regularly develop new products, they can develop a sizable inventory. What can be dangerous is when the resulting inventory shows up on the financial statements as an asset.

Good demand-and-supply planning processes impact your company every day—every purchase of raw material or outside service, the level of labor you employ, how you utilize your plants, warehouses, suppliers, and other resources. These are the daily habits that drive many outcomes for a company.

Your processes may need help if you find:

- There are no reports showing excess and obsolete (E&O) inventory.

- There is no process to examine existing E&O levels or to develop countermeasures to prevent such balances in the future.

- Product managers or marketing managers are not held accountable for remaining inventory levels after a new product roll-out.

- Aging inventory is not measured or reported on regularly.

If you don't track excess and obsolete inventory for new products, or if you don't hold your managers accountable for aged inventory, then *you may have an asset you cannot convert into cash.* What is worse, you may have processes and an organizational design in place that will continue to create this obsolete inventory (time to tap into those insights on segmentation and analyzing inventory shared in Chapter Two).

3. Are you relying on legacy IT systems that aren't serving? Growth often requires alterations and upgrades to the IT/ERP systems. If your company's IT system is built on legacy systems, was homegrown, has been modified, or is not utilizing current versions of databases and platforms, then it may be difficult to modify the systems to enable the growth in whatever form it takes.

Another side risk is that the cost to maintain older systems can go up dramatically. As the pool of programming expertise fades for a dated platform, the programmers become scarce and can charge exorbitant rates.

One of our PE clients was evaluating a target company for acquisition. The company relied on a system built on antiquated software and databases. By identifying this issue in diligence, our client was able to negotiate appropriate relief, complete the deal, and implement a robust system.

In Chapter One we considered some of the ways companies can make their IT system irrelevant or an expensive trinket. This risk looks at the other side of that coin: *Is your system ready to scale with you?*

4. Do you have adequate, or any, disaster recovery plans? All companies should have documented plans to deal with natural disasters, power outages, supplier chain interruptions, server crashes, currency fluctuations, cybercrime and other exceptions. Do you have documented plans for these?

At the very least, you should have a clear plan to address a computer system failure. Does your plan:

- Address redundant systems and automated offsite backups?

- Have reserve programmers and external resources?

- Responses to cybercrime?

  » Conduct an annual assessment
  » Conduct penetration tests
  » Hold sufficient cyber security insurance
  » Incident recovery plans

Earlier we mentioned the risks associated with relying on a sole supplier. It may make sense to have one supplier (keep all your eggs in one basket, then watch that basket!) AND we can take steps to ensure we're not exposed. Some suppliers have multiple factories, for example.

5. Are you compliant with relevant regulations, certifications, and accepted practices? How do you know?

As companies grow, they find it harder to fly under the radar. A small entrepreneurial company may not attract an OSHA visit. One idea to consider is to bring in an insurance and risk management expert. They will review your company's exposure to risk and the adequacy of your insurance to protect the company from those risks.

Expert hint: PE firms *always* bring in an insurance and risk service provider before they buy a company.

In light of our global economy, one source to consider is the Foreign Corrupt Practices Act (FCPA). For companies doing business across country borders, there are regulations that govern ethical practices. If any of the following good practices are missing, there needs to be more investigation:

- The company has a formal chief compliance officer (not necessarily a full-time position, just a clear compliance "owner" in the company). If your company is public, then this officer should have direct access to the audit committee.

- The company has a documented FCPA code of conduct, and training in that code is tracked by the employee.

  A major global industrial products manufacturer had poor international freight controls in place and asked us to help them de-risk the situation. They were exposed to risks related to non-compliance with FCPA and to potential litigation which would have caused significant additional expense and unwelcome media coverage. Deciding to address this risk through re-sourcing their freight needs and putting appropriate controls in place, the company actually reduced their annual expenditure by 25 percent—over $10 million!

Addressing early-stage versus late-stage risk

With my deepest respect for anyone who has gone through a debilitating condition or experienced it through a loved one, I'm going to share an analogy in the spirit of the organization as a dynamic organism.

Early detection is critical for many medical conditions such as cancer, cardiovascular disease, diabetes, HIV/AIDS, glaucoma, and Alzheimer's. Studies show that cancer typically follows a path from stage 1 to stage 4. Depending on the type of cancer, if caught early the treatment can be effective and focused, and 90–98 percent of people survive. Even when the cancer goes undetected until stage 3, there is a 70 percent survival rate overall. When action is delayed until stage 4, that survival rate, with all our medical knowledge and resources available today, plummets to 20 percent[14].

From my vantage point, companies—unlike people—rarely suffer a negative event that could not have been predicted to some degree. Whether or not your company is experiencing an issue with risk management right at this moment, it's prudent to keep the following in mind:

Addressing early-stage risks will often require little capital, and the changes will actually improve everyone's lives, services levels, and profitability along the way.

- Map your current processes, eliminate unnecessary steps, improve the process, and then document it.

- Develop a standard approach and then make it the norm—followed by all!

- Define what "good" looks like and measure that! Use effective leading and lagging metrics.

- As you go, build the habits and processes that will prepare your company to expose future risk in its early stages.

- Develop a good onboarding program. Get good at training new people in how to run some aspect of your business. This might seem like a random idea. It isn't. Reliance on tribal knowledge might be the prevailing risk, which is something we often see in companies. We all know turnover is coming, but we're rarely ready.

Addressing late-stage risks often requires bringing in a subject matter expert, devoting potentially overwhelming resources, and radical change. There will likely be a deadly threat at your door, forcing you to do whatever it takes to survive (as we saw with Peerless Products). Doing what you have done in the past will not yield different results now.

This will be a war, and it will be expensive. In the PE world, it often results in the company surviving, but in the end someone else will own it.

In both early- and late-stage cases you might seek an expert assessment to reveal what is really going on within the operations of your company, even when the financials don't indicate trouble, but you have seen the warning signs outlined in this section.

Here's another way to look at it: An old Fram Oil commercial plays on the phrase, "Pay me now or pay me later: Either buy a $2 oil filter now, or pay $2,000 to rebuild your engine later."

Great commercial, great lesson!

To get you started, here is a handy checklist that highlights risk factors we often uncover for our clients:

- The client doesn't know their E-mod rate (workman's comp modifier) or if it is above 1.

- Do people and visitors wear required safety equipment sometimes?

- Do the aisles sometimes have inventory in them (they're full!)?

- The client hasn't had a compliance audit. If someone asked us them to prove compliance with relevant regulations, could they?

- If the supply chain is interrupted, would they have to look for another option or source?

- Cybersecurity insurance. If the response is, *what is this*, then the client needs to look into it!

- Is there a management succession plan in place?

- Does the client make more profit when the cost of materials goes down, but they do not issue price increases when they go up?

- Quality levels vary based on the shift, location, or team working the line.

- The normal approach to onboarding new workers is on-the-job training.

- Customer complaints are increasing.

- More than 90 percent of the sales are with products introduced to the market years ago.

- The company could be susceptible to an ICE (Immigration and Customs Enforcement) audit.

Consider getting a "checkup" for early risk detection by having a conversation with subject matter experts in these areas:

- Financial, tax, and/or cost accounting audit

- Cybersecurity and insurance

- Environmental, OSHA, FDA, and worker safety

- Intellectual property and legal

- IT risk (outside of cybersecurity)

- Disaster recovery

- Marketing, customer concentration, disruptive technologies

- Global currency

Big picture upside

> **You will never address a risk you don't know exists.**

We've seen how risk can hide unnoticed until it becomes a major problem, so awareness that the risk exists is essential. And you'll never unleash that Black Gold if you don't know it's there—the Jed Clampett method of finding oil by mistake is not recommended!

Stay open to awareness of the possibility of external or internal risk. Overcome the temptation to avoid it or bury it under the rug in order to "protect" the company or yourself—or it CAN and WILL come back to bite you in some form or another, at some time or another!

Besides, *why would you avoid risk if you have seen how it could set you on the path to increase your profit?*

Instead, recognize and accept risk and entertain the possibility of positive outcomes. Be transparent with your team and stakeholders, as you join forces to investigate—you want to know if the juice is worth the squeeze and that addressing this risk will work.

Help is on the way! The chapters in Section II explore how you can leverage data, conversations, observations, and analyses to help your entire organization feel good about change.

Armed with this intel, take prudent steps to inoculate your company, prepare recovery plans, and build up your immune system. Welcome participation in its remediation, including thinking outside the system and releasing commitment to how "things were always done."

Read on to see how addressing risk can be a game-changer, not a game-killer! You'll see how you as a leader can prepare your organization—its culture and teams—to address any risk head-on, work together on solutions with fresh thinking and great KPIs, and take ownership of the changes your company needs to make in order to enjoy Shocking Profits!

Add value by reducing risk: Bottom line

➡ Risk is inherent in business transactions. Become aware of potential undisclosed risks, assess those situations, and see how you can take purposeful action to mitigate the risk *plus* find hidden value!

➡ With early awareness comes a better chance of planning for, and addressing, risky business. The cure tends to be non-invasive, low-cost, and effective. And the secondary (and often overlooked) benefit is that eliminating risk will provide collateral benefit in seemingly unrelated areas.

➡ Questions to ask to help uncover risk:

1. Does your company rely on tribal knowledge?
2. Do assets on the books not live up to the label?
3. Are you relying on legacy IT systems that aren't serving?
4. Do you have adequate, or any, disaster recovery plans?
5. Are you compliant with relevant regulations, certifications, and accepted practices? How do you know?

Shocking Leadership

WHY IS IT THAT ONCE we identify a problem or an opportunity, we assume everybody is with us, nobody's against us, and our people will hop right on board our bandwagon to take action?

When you think about it, how ridiculously untrue this assumption is in real life! It is a big expectation and a dangerous assumption for a leader to make about their people. It's also an unfair and impossible mandate for stakeholders to require of their leadership.

In Section I we studied how to become aware of hidden risk and latent value. We learned that awareness is necessary to change, but it is not enough.

Section II delves into the preparation necessary to turn that hidden value you have found into Shocking Profit! Change—I like to call it "transformation"—requires leadership that enrolls and guides people to accept its benefits (the size of the prize) and lays the groundwork toward reaching a worthy future state. Some say that leading your company to accept change is the hardest part of the journey—I know for sure it is often the most overlooked!

"A leader takes people where they want to go. A great leader takes people where they don't necessarily want to go, but ought to be." ~ Rosalynn Carter, former first lady of the United States

Here is a quick summary of what you will learn in each chapter of this transformational section.

1. Chapter Seven is about who you have to be to lead transformational change. *What are the leadership practices that will instill trust, a sense of safety, and a readiness to embrace change in your team?* These are the puzzle pieces that will build a problem-solving culture.

2. Chapter Eight is about building the business case. *How will you bring everyone along the change path with a shared belief* that there is a problem worth solving or a vision that needs to be attained? There's a way to do this that will alienate your team—there is another way that will produce excitement, openness, and engagement!

3. Chapter Nine is about preparing for action. *What are your next steps to engineer the future state you want to reach?* You'll leverage the business case to select a focus area, prepare the team that will move it forward, and clarify the end game to support and fund it.

Acceptance

Scene 2: A new direction.
Accepting the need to change

BOB, THE CEO OF ALPHA, invited Greg from our ProAction team to tour the facility and study the operation. Despite the improvements, they weren't in a position to meet the demand. Alpha was also unable to invest meaningful capital in new equipment or facilities. They had to see what more could be done with what they already had.

Greg walked the line, performed time studies, and mapped the process. He interviewed dozens of people from the operators to the CFO. The symptoms were rough—the operation was not balanced. The company carried $2.7 million in work-in-process inventory, clogging a third of their floor space. The dust collector, essential for safety, broke down almost every week, hobbling the operation. Scheduling was complicated and required the full-time attention of one of their sharpest technicians.

The operators took pride in their workmanship but produced scrap at every step, accounting for nearly 10 percent of partially finished goods. During our tours, Kevin, the plant manager, kept getting pulled away to solve issues on one line or another, and finally asked a colleague to finish the tour.

Technical fixes, layout changes, and a new approach would relieve the symptoms, but would not address the real problem. Kevin was personally jumping from one fix to another. He was a walking book of institutional knowledge! He knew the equipment, he had the experience, and he cared. But he couldn't do it all.

The good news was that Alpha had more demand than they could keep up with. They won the sales but couldn't deliver. They HAD to make major changes or destroy their reputation. This is the second-worst problem you can have. They were motivated to change. The mapping, interviews and clarity on the costs of the current approach provided a push. The tools and expertise we brought in gave the leadership team the confidence to embrace change.

One of my favorite memories throughout this whole experience was talking to Bob as we signed our agreement to work together. He was concerned about Kevin. "Bob, soon we'll be shipping 100,000 units per month, without burning Kevin out. Kevin will have an army of problem solvers and the ability to lead. He'll be able to go home and have dinner with his family."

To be continued ...

CHAPTER SEVEN

Setting the Stage for Change— Seven Leadership Secrets

Do not be afraid to be a leader. Do not be afraid to be less of a leader.

SHOCKING STATEMENT? ALLOW ME TO explain. We'll talk in this chapter about why and what it takes for you to step into a leadership position to uncover and leverage the hidden value in your company.

Don't worry, I don't intend to compete with the many great leadership books out there that teach you everything there is to know about being an exceptional leader (although what we cover in this chapter will definitely contribute to greatness). My focus is to call out the leadership practices I actually see in the companies we work with today, and the leadership strengths and skills which support a problem-solving culture that implements transformational change!

As leaders, we first have to work through the fears, egos, habits, worldviews, and simple lack of understanding to get our people to want to take action. This is not a bad thing. It's human nature. It's good that people don't simply accept every new idea—fearing the unknown is self-protective, and healthy skepticism can be valuable.

"Change? No, thank you." Once we showed the Fishy Business Company how they could deliver to Costco and Sam's Club without building a new factory or buying any new equipment (and make more money doing it), you might logically conclude that everyone was jumping at the chance to act on this new data and perspective.

That's not how it went down! It took time and leadership to get the organization to embrace this shift and get on board.

What could be blocking them from jumping on this incredible opportunity? Well, you might remember George, the nephew of the owner. He was fiercely proud of what his uncle had built (as he should be) and couldn't *conceive* of the idea that some consultants who had never in their lives felt fish slime on their hands could nearly double the output of his factory, let alone in eight weeks. We were also up against a number of veteran supervisors who were passionate about how they ran their lines and seemed to be holding an impossibly high bar by which to evaluate any change they might sign on to.

Of course, this is common. Once the team becomes **aware** of the issues, they're not yet ready to **accept** the change.

This was a company 60 days away from losing their two largest customers, thereby more than fifty percent of their revenue. Their backs were against the wall. The *only* reason we were able to help these clients make progress (a bumpy road, for sure) was the panic and fear around imminent, inevitable catastrophic loss. Effective in this case, but NOT the recommended approach to transformational change!

Overcoming blocks to taking action is a big deal. Trying to go from *awareness* to *action* is like running straight to third base without touching second—you're going to be called out every time. You have to touch second base to score a run. Second base is the metaphoric step of acceptance.

Acceptance is the work of bringing your people on board to a change project (or, for that matter, any vision). It's a piece of the progress puzzle which I notice company leaders often forget.

We all know that the only constant in life is change. But change is hard. It's scary. According to McKinsey & Company, 70% of companies' change projects fail![15]

In my career, I've witnessed my share of change efforts, including those which failed, faltered, or never even got out of the gate. Why did these outcomes happen? *Impending change can cause great resistance, fear, and confusion in a company—bottom up and top down.*

Taking charge of change

No surprise, taking charge of change starts with leadership—YOU. The seeds of change have been planted, and it is you as the leader who must feed the fertile ground for your people to enthusiastically share the company's goals and do their best work in a sustained and empowered way.

Any transformational growth opportunity will go nowhere unless you can lead the people you've brought together to implement it. You're the one who has the big-picture view and context that your employees may not be privy to. You have the vision, you know the stakes, you know the prize.

> **You know what to do—who do you have to BE before you can DO it?**

Let's explore how you, as the chief developer of people, cultivate a culture open to change.

Elevate your role from chief producer to grower of leaders

Executives in most cases have risen through the ranks based on their ability to perform and produce, right? They may not have been trained in leadership or people-management skills, but they know how to produce. Once they reach a management-level position, their responsibilities shift to leading an entire department, plant, company, or corporation.

The requirements of this new leadership position change dramatically!

Not surprisingly, many very able leaders we work with haven't made the shift from doing to leading. Ultimately, they're not getting change or continuous improvement done—and definitely not inspiring a happy, more productive workplace.

> **"The Whack-a-Mole King."** Alex, the GM of Fantastic Food-Pack, was powering through. He was often the first one in the plant and the last to leave, working hard to hold everything and everyone together.

Alex was the most physically intimidating man I've ever met—6 foot 6, well over 300 pounds of muscle, a former Navy Seal. Until recently his hobby had been MMA fighting. He stopped the sport when others complained that the bruises on his face were distracting in the workplace! Alex was also one of the most sincere and best-intentioned people I know. As GM he liked to build consensus with his team and would get personally involved when a team member could not, or did not, complete their daily work well.

Both admirable and ineffective at the same time ...

On top of being the fifth GM in as many years, Alex was contending with a myriad of issues rippling out from bugs in the implementation of a new ERP system. He spent much of his time dealing with these issues that popped up daily, like playing Whack-a-Mole and not winning any tickets to turn in for a prize!

He was exhausted and stressed, but felt he owed it to his team to hold it all together. He was a good man, yet he was not *leading*—he was *producing*, and it was unsustainable for him and the company.

We were called in because the company was incurring almost $150,000 in monthly scrap ($1.7 million per year). For a $35-million division, this was a problem. In addition, they had lost several major customers after consecutive periods of poor performance.

From our work together, they got back to profitability and calm—within three months!

How were we able to reverse course so quickly after years of struggle and poor performance? Well, we found the fences and learned why they were erected ... **the root cause was leadership.**

Alex was a producer, not a leader. With his big heart he would try to lift his people by doing the parts of their jobs they struggled with. As a result, *Alex had unwittingly taught his team to rely on him instead of on themselves.* Millions of variations of symptoms can erupt from this situation, causing the producer to play Whack-A-Mole as each of them pops up and screams for attention.

Leaders like Alex need to learn how to *be a grower of leaders.* If you take on all the problems and initiatives that arise in the company, you're robbing your team of the chance to learn to do it themselves. Sorry to say, you, the leader, become the bottleneck to progress!

When you master leadership development you help your people improve the business. And I'm happy to say you then get to go play another round of golf, vacation in Hawaii, or find a company to buy. Yes, you WILL have more time (more on this in Chapter Eleven)!

The seven secrets to cultivating a culture open to change

In my experience working with thousands of CEOs, the most lasting, sustainable, ethical profitability happens for CEOs who do not declare mandates and jam change down their people's throats.

Instead, they provide clarity, a sense of safety, and a team spirit which focuses on the problem, not the person. They also help empower and inform their people and provide the tools and authority needed to accomplish the change effort successfully.

> **Remember, you, the leader, feed the fertile ground for your people to take charge of change.**

Emulating these seven secrets will help you develop a team that is emotionally prepared to:

- Accept and align themselves around change

- Examine data and see where it leads them

- Have the courage to think creatively about new, better ways to do things

- Feel empowered to take prudent action.

If you're committed to building TOWARD something, then you want to set the right tone in your company through your own habits and behaviors, which will ripple outward from you, to management, and to everyone else! Your goal is to nurture an environment in which your people feel safe and supported to do all the things I just described—as a matter of habit.

You want them to know their roles, their boundaries, and how they will be evaluated. They want to know you have their back. If not, they will be reading the tea leaves rather than blazing a trail.

SECRET #1:
Have a shared vision

In 1962, President John F. Kennedy visited NASA for the first time. During his tour of the facility, he met a janitor who was carrying a broom down the hallway. The President casually asked the janitor what he did for NASA, and the janitor replied, "I'm helping put a man on the moon."[16]

Know and define your "why." What is the reason your company exists? What particular customer need do you serve? If you sell chickens, what makes you different? Who would have thought that people would pay $3–$4 *more* for a dozen eggs just because the chickens were allowed to roam a pasture and eat natural food?! We live in a transformational economy. More than ever before, knowing the meaning and purpose of what you do is relevant to staying competitive in the marketplace.

Understanding why your company exists is also crucial to effectively motivate and engage your workforce around a meaningful purpose. Leadership needs to know it before they can translate it for their people.

There are many excellent resources (and coaches) that help companies define and embed their "why" and core values. Whichever approach you use, the point I want to impress upon you is that you, as the leader, provide the vision for your company—it's an important and exciting opportunity you don't want to miss!

SECRET #2:
Give your people clarity

For people to know what they need to accomplish in their role, they must understand where the company is going, where they fit in, and how to measure their personal success.

"Clear is kind. Unclear is unkind."
—Brené Brown[17]

Brené Brown's studies have revealed that clarity is so important in "the way we talk to each other to the way we negotiate with external partners. It's simple but transformative." What this looks like for you, the CEO, is: You engage with your people in a candid, honest way, in the tough conversations as well as the easy ones, in naming the problems, and in giving clear, productive feedback.

The "kind" part of clarity is that when you're candid and transparent, you're being kinder to your people than dishonoring them by avoiding the truth or trying to protect them from problems. Communications delivered in kindness honor the spirit of working together. This type of clarity enables people to:

- *Understand their roles*, boundaries, and what success looks like

- *Be more flexible and creative* because you have given them safety, trust, and "permission" to engage

- *Know where they fit* into the company's vision and goals

- *Know where they stand* with you.

Communicating with clarity also offers *you* more clarity about your people, so that you have the knowledge and flexibility to make great decisions on their behalf.

Your company likely has some core values that underpin it. Defining, articulating, and practicing a clear set of core company values—and then LIVING those values—are critical for successful change. This is the foundation for acceptance, belonging, and **trust**. People need to trust in their company when they're about to take part in an uncertain future.

From personal experience I can share how transformational Secret #2 is. In 2015, my partners and I defined our core values, following the EOS methodology[18]. We tried them on; we tested them. In the end we loved them. They define us. They're proudly listed on our company homepage. Over the years, we have hired, promoted, and fired people based on these core values. Our team operates as if ProAction is a cause, not just a company or a job, and as a result we make a good profit. Developing and living our company values is one of the great joys of my life. Trust me on this one.

SECRET #3:
Hire, promote, and fire based on company core values

"If you are thinking about letting someone go,
you should have already done it."
—David Kreilein, *CEO of Sunnen Products Company*

Have you ever been part of a group conversation that felt like musicians jamming, seamlessly making beautiful music—then one more person entered the group and the music stopped?

There is disturbance in the Force! People start to feel self-conscious and reluctant to share. They're on their heels.

Yes, you hire and promote people because of their experience and technical skills. What's often missing in this picture are **attitude, aptitude, and values.** Hire and promote people who can competently carry out their role, who want to fill that role AND who live your core values. This is not to say everyone thinks the exact same way or will always agree. It means there is alignment and compatibility with the company's foundational core values and vision.

Not only will you benefit from the energy and leadership of that person, but the whole team will function more harmoniously!!

By the same token, fire people based on their NOT being aligned with your core values. It sounds harsh, but a person who is out of sync with the company's values can drain everyone's energy and block smooth progress. Yet I've seen where the company keeps them on, even when they're not working out. These situations have a significant negative impact on morale; people notice that leadership tolerates mediocrity and behavior that's against the company's values—this can be a real trust-breaker.

We had to make this choice ourselves at ProAction. One of our teammates was hitting his numbers, he was productive—and he could stop our harmonious "jam" at the drop of a hat! He was a good man, but had different values that led him to do and say things that would distract the team and prevent progress.

It was interesting to notice how once he moved on (to a better situation for him, I'm happy to report), the energy at ProAction shifted in a positive way and made everyone feel safe again. My company truly lives its values and people can count on our consistency, even in the face of losing an otherwise productive team member.

SECRET #4:

Get in touch with the actual place where the work gets done in your company

If you're not connected to the work that your company is doing, the value of your strategic understanding is wasted—and your people will know it. Here is a quick quiz to help you gauge where you stand with your people. Ask yourself:

1. *If I ran into one of my line workers in the grocery store, would they say* hi *to me? Would I recognize them?*

2. *Does the second shift janitor know how their job fits into the vision of the company?*

3. *When I, or a member of my leadership team, lead a tour through the factory, do I encourage the visitors to ask the workers questions directly, or do I need to control the message?*

4. *When was the last time I worked a shift on the line? When was the last time I walked the line?*

5. *Does my team have twenty years of experience, or have they repeated one year of experience twenty times?*

Let's call in "going to Gemba" to help you out here. The way to keep your bird's-eye perspective on your company is to walk the line. In whatever leadership role you may hold, make it a HABIT to spend time with the people who do the work.

When you take the lead in walking the line, not only does it put you in touch with your operations to solve problems, your presence emanates throughout the company. *Your employees see you and are inspired by you.* It also sends a message to the CFO, VP of Ops, VP of Sales, etc., to make it a regular practice themselves—a powerful way that a leader can develop leaders!

SECRET #5:
Replace judgment with curiosity

Being a leader involves giving your people every opportunity to take part in the *solution of a problem*—this is a foundational piece of a problem-solving culture. If people feel they're being judged and analyzed in every interaction, they're not going to feel safe about speaking up. You want them to bring up the problems and share their mistakes or "failures," so your team can work together on them. "I'm with you on this. It's OUR problem, let's figure it out."

You seek information and knowledge with curiosity. No one is looking for who's at fault. You start with the assumption that everybody has earned their way here—"we're all in this together!" In fact, when there's a "mistake" or "fail" we're actually excited ...

> *Holy cow, we found an opportunity to do something better.*
> *What does "better" look like?*
> *What's the systemic issue that will reveal the root cause of the problem?*
> *What are some creative solutions we can try out?*

SECRET #6:
Talk less. Talk last. Ask Why? Why? Why?

Why is it important to talk less and speak last? Easy answer: **If you tell your people the answer, they will never develop into leaders!**

> *"The CEO should always be the last to speak.*
> *If you speak first, you shut down the conversation."*
> —David Cancel, *CEO of Drift1*

When the CEO opens their mouth, they shut off all other thinking in the room—it's a natural phenomenon about authority. So, when you're leading a group, avoid letting your view be known until everyone else shares.

Think of yourself as a conductor of an orchestra, not a one-man band. The conductor only makes beautiful music when everyone is playing together. Put your accordion, cymbal, and harmonica away. Give the violins, brass, and bongos space to fill the room with music!

Give your team room to air their own ideas and solutions. You might learn something, such as a better solution than your own. You then have the choice to either go along with what they suggested or provide direction in a different direction. In any case, you have supported and energized them by giving them recognition and constructive feedback.

You're acting in your role as a developer of leaders! In doing so, everyone wins.

The best way to avoid talking—and gain much in return—is to ask good questions. One simple question is, *Why*? The "Five Whys" is a well-known management technique you can learn more about in the *Go Deeper Appendix*. It's a simple method that can effectively get to the root of a problem or cause. When you see something unexpected, good, or bad, ask why.

Asking questions from curiosity, not judgment, engages your people, gets to the bottom of issues, circulates ideas, stirs imagination and sparks innovation.

SECRET #7:
Take on a "shake 'em up" mindset

Being a developer of leaders requires fresh thinking and creativity. You want to find out things like:

> *Where do I have a vision worth pursuing?*
> *What will it take to realize that vision?*
> *Who do I need to take us there?*
> *In what areas can I replace myself?*

You get to shake things up—to become the "troublemaker!" You might have to break stuff that ain't broke—not for chaos' sake, but to get out of a stale status-quo mediocrity and reveal a more creative and innovative way.

You as the CEO get to set the tone for your company and team to try new things rather than stick with what has always been done. The single most common response we get when we ask clients why something is the way it is? Some version of *well, that was how I was taught* or, *that's how it's always been.* My happiest moments are when I get to turn that attitude on its head!

How to be a Champion of Change for your team: The problem-solving culture

These seven leadership secrets are the foundation of what I mentioned earlier—a problem-solving culture which implements transformational change. Thoughtful, innovative change and continuous improvement happen as a result of the collective effort. Purposeful change is what keeps a company thriving in the market and for its people.

The problem-solving culture is at the heart of the Shocking Profit story!

> **A problem-solving culture is a blame-free, collaborative exploration of solutions.**

Anyone can approach a tactical problem ... you find someone to fix it or fix it yourself, get it done, and walk away. A problem-solving culture led by a champion of change pulls together a team, and works through the awareness, acceptance, and action model to thoroughly look at the problem or opportunity as a transformational exercise.

You enable, teach, and support your team to solve problems themselves, and give them the tools, resources, and authority to make the change—and then you get out of the way. We're moving from just tactical. It's no longer a continuous Whack-a-Mole game; in fact, you're finding a new permanent home for the moles, so whacking is eliminated! You're leading a change for the future of your company.

In the next few chapters, we'll go deeper into what a problem-solving culture looks like, and how it forms the habits of your team centered around transformation change.

Big picture upside

We can change this world if we understand the great joy—and solemn responsibility—of leadership, to look at those people under our care and help them have a successful life. We want them to share their gifts, be appreciated for doing so, and go home to whatever their family situation is with a sense that they matter.

The ideas in this chapter (and in fact, throughout the book) are not just tactics to pull more productivity out of people. They're not cost-cutting techniques. These lessons bring alignment to the company and nurture a culture that brings out the best in people. And in doing so, the company functions at its best, as does each individual within it.

EBITDA (or think of it as a proxy for the cash flow generated by the business) is an easy way to keep score of success, yet is woefully incomplete. Profitability is a great outcome, but a poor target on its own.

What we're talking about is the intersection of productivity and the employee's engagement, well-being, and morale. My wish for your company is to improve daily habits, approaches, processes, and use of equipment and technology *AND to become excellent through helping your people become excellent.*

Seven leadership secrets: Bottom line

➡ Do not be afraid to be a leader. Do not be afraid to be less of a leader. Elevate your role from chief producer to grower of leaders.

➡ Seven leadership secrets to cultivating a culture open to change:

＊ Have a shared vision.

＊ Give your people clarity.

＊ Hire, promote, and fire based on company core values.

＊ Get in touch with the actual place where the work gets done in your company

＊ Replace judgment with curiosity.

＊ Talk less. Talk last. Ask Why? Why? Why?

＊ Take on a "shake 'em up" mindset.

➡ Be a Champion of Change for your team! You enable, teach, and support your team to solve problems themselves, and give them the tools, resources, and authority to make the change—and you get out of the way.

CHAPTER EIGHT

Wake Up Your Team—To Their Power, Potential, and Value

AS FAR AS I CAN tell, few people look forward to hard work. Change means that people will have to leave the comfort of the current situation and jump into one they simply don't know. It feels scary, risky, and often looks like it's going to be tough going. However, buried deep in that perspective lie the exciting opportunity, innovation, engagement, improvement, and achievement they can experience from thoughtful change.

Your mandate is to help them discover this!!

> *"Opportunity is often dressed up to look like hard work."*
> —Attributed to Thomas Edison

You, the CEO, recognize the potential outcome of mining the Black Gold hidden in your company—you can imagine (even *taste*) the size of the prize. ***Now you have to get people to agree to something they didn't know existed ten minutes ago,*** and which may go against how they've seen the company run for the last five, ten, or twenty years.

Do you remember learning about Newton's Laws of Motion in grade school? The first one is the Law of Inertia[19]. A body at rest tends to stay at rest and a body in motion tends to stay in motion. I love that a law of physics is not just physically but figuratively true—and inertia in companies is real!

You know that when your company has the momentum to overcome the status quo, you will find infinite resources to help you succeed. You now have valuable leadership habits to practice and support you in developing your people to take appropriate action with enthusiasm and excellence. So now ...

> **How do you help your people accept that the opportunities you identify are worth seeking?**

In order to shift out of the comfort of the known and into the embrace of change, your people need to:

- *Feel they're valued and respected* by the company—and that their input matters. They need to be heard.

- *Hear the truth*—yes, they CAN handle the truth! If they understand the purpose of the change, the "why" and the data supporting it, they will be more apt to embrace the process (and the change that will follow).

- *Trust in the CEO* and management teams that the change is not a disguised ploy to get rid of them.

- *Believe they're empowered* (or about to be) to see the change through. They will feel safe in a problem-solving culture.

A key component of building any relationship is good communication, and it's CRUCIAL for bringing your people along to understand, trust, and accept your company's vision. Not just communicating to your leadership team and management and hoping it trickles down to the rest of the employees; instead, as my friend Mark Panico[20] advises, "up and down through the ranks—to build trust and support for any change agenda." His rule of thumb is the widely-embraced wisdom: "Just when you think you have said it enough, say it again."

Mark shared his experience with me: "As a CEO, getting small groups of employees together for informal lunch time Q&As has always been extremely helpful. It builds trust and I was able to learn about what was going on in the business that wasn't filtered up and learn how my messages were being received."

Start. Get more intentional about how to communicate often and strategically with everyone in your organization, especially the production-line people who typically rarely get a chance to spot management, let alone hear from them.

Six steps to investigate opportunity indicators

Let's explore how to work with your management team on digging into those "opportunity indicators" you uncovered in Section I, with common goals to thoroughly and systematically:

- *Figure out whether or not the warning signs* highlight waste or are simply an anomaly.

- *Analyze the data* that will likely (trust me, it will!) support some kind of improvement initiative.

- *Create a persuasive case* for change or improvement to present to the rest of the company.

- *Gear up your teams* for an exciting ride!!!

Here are the steps to kick off this assessment, while enrolling your team to join with you as Champions of Change:

1. **Assign a champion**

2. **Get to the truth: Go to Gemba**

3. **Quantify and clarify the truth**

4. **Synthesize the assessment.**

5. **Present an irresistible business case for the proven path**

6. **Lay the foundation for agreement and action**

1. Assign a champion.

Before we build the case, pick someone from your team to own the assessment process. If you're noticing a theme, you're right—you're not going to be THE problem solver. Rather, we're *preparing you to develop a team of problem solvers, who then train others.* This can start by selecting a leader within your company to be responsible for and committed to this step of investigating what needs attention as well as creating a collective sense of urgency.

Assigning a project champion will support your efforts to:

- *Invest focused leadership* on these important issues

- *Develop that champion* to lead change going forward

- *Demonstrate to the whole organization* that others (besides you) are empowered to drive change

- *Overcome resistance* to moving away from the status quo

- *Prepare for sustainable momentum*

- *Problem solve, as a team*

- *Build a change culture*

The rest of these steps will apply to your champion, to you, and to those invited to participate.

2. Get to the truth: Go to Gemba

I'm calling up again my favorite and often-underutilized weapon of going to Gemba! We touched upon it with Leadership Secret #4, and I'm levelling it up here for you to take the lead in this assessment and show your people how it's done! What's required, in essence, is walking the factory floor, observing what's happening and talking to the people who are directly involved in doing the work. By this time, you should be getting an idea of how this works from the descriptions and examples you've read so far.

I can promise this: You cannot sit in a conference room and think you're going to figure out where the improvement and opportunities lie. The process MUST include going to where the work is being done. *And you CANNOT awaken your team until you have met them where they live—right where the action is happening.*

Going to Gemba may take you and/or your leadership team out of your comfort zone—that's a good thing! A few things happen here: You all get to learn what's actually going on. The people who work in those departments or shop floors get to be heard. Incredible outcomes occur! "Bob" or "Jane" recommends that this line needs to be moved, it turns out to be acted upon, and the results are higher productivity, leaner inventory, higher profits. You see how proud your people are of the work they do and their potential to take ownership of their part in a carefully planned improvement initiative.

Make your assessment comprehensive and valuable with these tips:

- *Show curiosity and an open mind.* Ask deep questions to get to the root of the issue, not to root out the guilty.

- *Observe* how the job is getting done and what the holdbacks or roadblocks might be. Conduct your observations via a systematic method and record-keeping.

- *Benchmark versus define your potential.* This is not the stage of finding answers; rather, you're quantifying those current-state points of reference against which you will make your recommendations for the future-state changes.

The observation process might look something like this, depending on the nature of your company or the opportunity indicators you're mining:

1. *Walk through the processes from order to delivery.* Staple yourself to an order to see how it's done. Ask someone in each department or floor to show you. And remember, any deficiencies are NOT a reflection of that worker, their competence, or effort. It's a reflection of the system and culture that they have been functioning in.

   When you complete these reviews you will see where the leaks are—the extra steps the worker must go through, the extra judgment calls and manual effort to make sure things are done right, waste, or inefficiencies—all of which might be impacting customer service.

2. *If your company holds inventory, take a cycle count.* Yes, you! Go get twenty items from the system and count what you find in the warehouse (pull in area supervisors and operators to help). When you don't find what the system says you should have, ask the others what they think is happening here. Pull that string and see where it goes!

3. *Pick your best problem solvers and ask them to dig in*—sharing with you what they believe the real issues are, and what they would do to fully understand the issue and root causes.

I'm going to repeat that term "systematic!" As you observe, interview, and survey employees, be sure you have set up a clear system to gather information methodically and objectively for the particular assessment you're conducting. You want to capture the core of the issues and understand them thoroughly and holistically so that—to the best of your ability—you have the data you'll need to make a sound decision.

When we at ProAction go on site, we work to understand how our client runs the company, including a little bit about why. In the process, we arrive at and share three types of observations:

1) **What they do well—and celebrate that.** We make sure we don't throw the baby out with the bathwater—whatever we come up with in the future has to recognize that what the company has been doing is already effective in a lot of ways. Also, an honest compliment shows people they're seen and appreciated for the work they're doing today.

2) **What the constraints are.** People often have to know that we understand what they're going through before they listen to

us. We always reflect what we see back to them before making comments or observations. We show understanding that the constraints are important and unique to their business.

We might say: "We know you're a union shop. Everything you ship out is custom designed; every order is different. You have very demanding customers, and a 24-hour lead time." By naming the current situations and constraints, people hear that we understand them and their situation. This establishes common ground, defends resistance, and builds trust.

Acknowledging constraints, or what the team may feel makes their situation unique, is imperative. Leaving this step out will lead people to ignore you because they think you don't get it (and maybe you don't).

The punchline: *This compassionate approach is just as important for your people internally as it is for us as the third-party consultant.*

3) Observations that lead to the recommendations. From our observations, we raise awareness of what is missing, wasteful, or dangerous, AND possibilities for improvement and change that will meet the desired goals. We're not announcing recommendations or mandates yet, just opening up minds to another possible way of thinking, such as: "I see your process for doing x and the workarounds your line has to do to meet the deadlines. Does this make your job harder? What else happens that gets in your way?"

Throughout the assessment and data-gathering, you show everyone you're interested and not judging, treat them with dignity, praise them for what they do well, identify the things they have to deal with, and note where improvements could be made.

This is laying the framework for getting *acceptance* that will lead to *action*. And, of course, this is simply the right and respectful way to treat your people, no matter what job they hold in your organization!

3. Quantify and clarify the truth.

Along with your interviews, surveys, and observations, your team is gathering quantitative information.

Metrics and mapping are absolutely critical! Ask:

> *How do we know if we are doing a good job?*
> *Do we know what success looks like?*
> *And, most importantly, how is it measured (or not)?*

Let's look at each of these in turn, so you can collect the data that will help your team identify the top two or three projects which will best serve your customers' needs!

About Metrics

As we explored in Chapter Five, metrics are a way to define what success looks like for our company. And we're able to review both lagging and leading indicators, comparing them to prior performance and among different groups.

Here are some of our favorite metrics and how we evaluate them.

Lagging indicators focus on the actual performance of our company. These demonstrate the impact of our strategy and processes. Judge the tree on its fruit! Examples you might want to review include:

- *Net income*

- *Free cash flow* (how much money the business generates after all investments, taxes, and interest payments)

- *Inventory turns*

- *Lead times*. Lead time can be considered a leading or a lagging indicator; in this case it measures the time it takes for your company to respond to customer demand, so it relates to a result. And it has the added gravitas of predicting future success.

At the end of the day, combining consistently high inventory turns and fast lead times is a feat only a high-performing company can achieve. And if you produce solid cash flow as a result, the company is sailing smoothly!

Leading indicators focus on predictive metrics that give us a sense of our behavior. Some of my favorite examples include:

- *Schedule attainment* (in other words, how much of what you predicted that you would get done today did you get done?)

- *The cost of poor quality.* What is the cumulative cost of scrap, rework, rejects, late deliveries, premium freight, and other waste?

- *Safety-related metrics.* How many days since a lost-time accident? What is your E-Mod rate? How often do your drivers exceed the speed limit?

- *Perfect order percentage.* What percentage of your orders are delivered on time, in full, with no errors or rejects?

- *What percentage of your employees do not show up* for their shift without approval?

- *How accurate is your inventory* in the system?

For each metric you review, consider the following to provide context:

- *Compare with prior performance.* How does your current performance compare to your best demonstrated levels? If you did it before, why can't you do it now?

- *Compare with other shifts, teams, divisions, and locations.* Variation is bad. When you see one shift, one operator, or one facility operating at a high level, you can mirror that in others (save for things like product mix that truly show you're doing something different).

- *Look at the patterns.* Similar to the first two methods, looking to see how performance differs based on different variables tells us something. Some customers are more profitable; some SKUs are easier to run. Look for data points outside of a healthy pattern.

- *Segment.* Look at your metrics and data by customer size, region, SKU volume, salesperson, facility, shift, time of day. This will show you patterns and where you make money and where you give it back!

- *Correlation/Causation.* When looking at patterns, evaluate whether two variables are simply related or if one causes the other.

- *Benchmarking.* When data is available, compare your results to other companies in your industry and in other industries.

We start our reviews by evaluating metrics and opportunities internal to the company. Benchmarking, in my opinion, should be relied upon to set floors (minimum acceptable levels)—never to set the ceiling. One example comes to mind. "Six Sigma" means that a company has less than 3.4 exceptions out of one million opportunities[21]. It implies a quality level of 99.9997%. That is high! But consider this, if the aerospace industry operated at that quality level, a plane would fall out of the sky every day. When we visit food manufacturing companies they may scrap over 10% of their ingredients. We get two lessons from this example:

1. You must take the industry into consideration to evaluate a benchmark.

2. You can challenge yourself to reach levels demonstrated in other industries.

These approaches are key to evaluating performance and prioritizing what to improve.

Make sure you're looking beyond the obvious indicator. Refer back to Chapter Five for examples of metrics to define, monitor, and manage.

Last piece of advice on metrics: You will be challenged to add new metrics, or to focus on one in isolation.

> *"Everything should be made as simple as possible.*
> *But not simpler."*
> —Attributed to Albert Einstein

I love this quote! So funny and so true. The moral is to guard against oversimplification. The steps outlined above will push you to look at context, to look at situations from different angles.

About Mapping

In some cases, you may want to formally map out some processes. I like to use a high-level Value Stream Map (VSM) with clients, a visual tool used in Lean management. On the simplest level, it helps clarify the flow of information and materials required to bring a product to a customer, which of course is the bottom-line goal of this entire effort.

To be sure, this is an involved process and requires participation from multiple people, preparation and time. So, I suggest you leverage an experienced Lean manufacturing expert in this process. The impact of having someone with the creativity, experience, and confidence to lead you through VSM is worth its weight in gold.

Here's how it works, beginning with some helpful definitions:

- *Cycle time:* the amount of time it takes to complete a task without any waiting, delays, quality problems or interruptions. If you have everything you need and work from start to finish, how long does it take?

- *Lead time:* the total elapsed time it takes in real life for an operation to be completed. This takes all waste, delays, interruptions, etc., into account.

- *Material flow:* shows the path that converts raw materials into your finished product.

- *Information flow:* In addition to showing how material flows through your process, the map will also document the flow of information.

- *Inventory:* the inventory associated with a step. In a front-office situation, this could refer to how many invoices are sitting in a person's inbox at a given time.

A shorter lead time leads to a more efficient process—that's the goal! *When you identify a longer cycle, you can be sure there is a bottleneck somewhere that's begging to be fixed or improved.*

"Mapping the Wrapping." Our client was the Willy Wonder Chocolate Company—how fortunate were we?? With the project champion and her team, we were mapping the cycle of a wrapped chocolate bar. Basically, it was tracking the cycle time from the cocoa bean to processing the chocolate to wrapping it in its packaging—an estimated total of about three hours. In reality, however, the time between the bean going into production and the time it was shipped had been about three-and-a-half months!

The mapping led us to some dramatic changes. When we developed the future state map, taking out waste and eliminating pauses in the process, we ended up reducing the overall lead time from 110 days to only 10! And, because this map was not created by consultants in a conference room but by the people who run that process every day, support for the change was already in place.

We have presented a big idea here on value stream mapping. There is enough here to trudge your way through it and get some nice wins. It is also an area with tremendous resources, from books and classes to state-sponsored facilitators and, I hear, some excellent consulting firms 😊!

> **Truth is not a stone meant to hurl at people.**

This is one of my favorite things to say when I introduce the topic of metrics and mapping to my clients. Why? Because people invariably begin to get uncomfortable when they think their work is getting measured. They believe they're being judged and that it's all about being right or wrong.

This is an assumption you want to dispel RIGHT OUT OF THE GATE.

"We can do it faster—we'll prove it!!" For an assessment at Chemicals-R-Us company, we aimed to measure on-time delivery by mapping the process. The shipping supervisor, Jackson, looked at me with wide eyes, saying emphatically, "You can't do that!" I responded, "Really? Why is that?" "Well, because sometimes the salespeople offer to deliver faster than we're capable of doing—they're supposed to tell the customer it takes a week to get there, and instead they promise delivery in three days. So, we shouldn't be held accountable!"

I calmed Jackson down: "Okay, I understand. The point here is not to judge you. The goal is to see if we're delivering when the client wants it. And if we're not, it starts a conversation. It could turn out to be something related to your shipping process, communication between departments, or vendor agreements."

We assured Jackson (as well as the salespeople) that we were NOT there to judge, blame, or fire—just to get to the root cause of any gaps in meeting customer agreements and to fix those gaps, together. The best way to do that is mapping—"just the facts, ma'am!"

In the end, we measured on-time delivery versus the date promised the customer. Jackson felt better about it after we experienced a problem-solving exercise in which we noted when customers requested shorter than promised lead times. Not only did they experience an improvement in on-time delivery, the discussion uncovered a pain point that caused bad blood. Salespeople were now aware of their impact on operations and were more thoughtful when they promised premium services.

Once you have systematically and thoroughly gathered input and data, what's next?

Most often, a few exciting opportunity threads or stark gaps in productivity will pop out pretty clearly. You may see two or three obvious "leaky pipe" indicators and opportunities—or 20 or 30!

4. Synthesize the assessment

In our client work, we compile a comprehensive report on what we have concluded. Organize your information around these considerations:

- *Observations*
  - » Outline what has been done well, what constraints are being faced, and the indicators of pain (we sometimes call these "the elephants in the room," issues that often get ignored).

- *Risks to address*
  - » Identify the early-stage and late-stage risks you found.
  - » Estimate the cost, time ,and effort required to address them.

- *Opportunities*

  » Outline the improvement opportunities that are emerging from the observations and risks.

  » Categorize them by functional area, product family, facility—whichever is most relevant.

  » Group them into a list of initiatives.

  Note: At this stage, simply make a list of all the ideas you have to improve. In the next chapter we'll talk about how to combine these ideas into a core set of actionable initiatives.

- *Financial impact*

  » Financial impact refers to the "steady state" earnings once the recommended changes have been fully implemented.

  » Show the ROI from addressing the risks and making the improvements, considering the impacts on:

    » Income
    » Balance sheet
    » Market position (this would include the impact on safety, employee engagement, lead times, and quality levels)

  » Summarize the complexity, level of control, timeline, and cost related to making the improvements and addressing the issues and risks.

- *Recommendations*

  » Weight the consequences and impacts of the list of initiatives and prioritize them, considering:

    » Strengths
    » Issues
    » Opportunity to improve/add value to the company

» Create a short list of initiatives to present to the company.

The executive summary

Next, we write an executive summary with the conclusions we have drawn. This is the Super Bowl kickoff that will communicate the analysis to the rest of the company with the strength of a clear, cohesive voice to get that championship ring!

> **The executive summary tells a positive story about the sustainable value the business can expect in a future-state scenario.**

This is NOT a repetition of each data point from the report. It is a narrative, *the story of what is going on in this company in its current state and what a future state might look like.* Describe briefly what you have discovered and are recommending, supported by the key facts, observations, and analyses from the report.

The executive summary allows everyone to start off on the same page—and get a good glimpse of the prize and its size!

For a detailed outline that we use at ProAction, refer to the *Go Deeper Appendix.*

Here are important points to consider:

1. Keep the summary to one or two pages.

2. Focus on the few items that are substantial. Resist the temptation to list everything you know. Make sure your content reflects what's in the report (no added material or editorializing).

3. Be sure you're differentiating observations and recommendations. Observations are facts, either accurate or not with little room for argument. Recommendations come later in the report and are inspired by the observations. For example, "We need to improve the quality system" is a recommendation. "On average, 2.6% of products coming off the line require rework before they can be shipped to a customer" is an observation.

4. Avoid any gratuitous or judgmental language. Model the language of a strong problem-solving culture!

5. Make the language appropriate for your audience. Avoid acronyms, jargon, and generic terms such as world-class, always, best, etc.

6. Present an irresistible business case for the proven path

The facts may give you a green light to go, yet the missing piece that will break inertia and spark momentum remains: *the emotional, intuitive component.* This involves the human experience of your company and the world it lives in and is a key part of a fantastically sound decision!

The goal here is to reach a balance—weighing the facts against the emotional—and taking into consideration the company's vision and values.

Working with this equation is not only important to sound decision making; it is also the foundation of the approach you're going to take to persuade the rest of the company.

"What would it mean to you?" Remember George's company, Mighty Tasty Meals? He and I were having a conversation about the potential to increase the value of his company by another $20 million in the next year, and what that would mean to him and his family. We also talked about the impact that the required changes would have on the lives of his employees. They would rise out of the firefighting culture and learn to work as a team to solve problems. I knew George well by this time, and I believed what was important to him was less about the dollars and more about his people. I wasn't entirely sure big profits mattered to him.

So, I approached him with this truth: "Right now, George, your people are in firefighting mode. They're tense. They're frustrated. They're not living their best lives. You're not leveraging their capabilities and potential. What would it be worth for you to know that you were leaving the company with your people well paid, learning, thriving, secure, and happy?"

George and I had that conversation on January 1st, 2024. We agreed that the real win in this project would be changing the life of his plant manager. Gone would be the long, stressful days.

By April of that same year, they were producing 80% more product with the same people and equipment. But what we marveled at was the change we'd hoped for in Kevin, his plant manager. No longer was he running from machine to machine, putting out fires, and personally expediting orders. He now relied on his team, they worked together to identify and solve problems. He was able to have dinner with his family almost every night!

To get clear on the proven path as well as set the hook, answer these questions with your team:

- *Is the intended financial and/or market impact meaningful to the company?*

- *Who else cares about this besides you?*

- *What would it mean to you personally if we solve this problem or reach this vision?*

- *What would it mean to you if we maintain the status quo?*

When the team is on board, the exciting work really begins—***and it takes the power away from the fear!***

Once you share the improvement initiative, you can expect people to say, "No, we can't ship in 24 hours," or "We can't do 20% more," or "There's no way we can reduce their cost" .... These are natural responses, and concerns and fears need to be addressed. This is when you, the CEO, become the "troublemaker" and push the point.

Lolly Daskal, founder of Lead From Within, a global leadership and consulting firm, recognized this about leaders. "Great leaders push people beyond their comfort zones while providing the support needed to make them comfortable."

When leaders push people to do something, it can work for a time, but people can become demotivated, too far out of their comfort zone, or demanding results (seeing-is-believing syndrome). This is the inflection point I refer to as bringing out the "leadership hammer." A hammer in the hands of an amateur can lead to a lot of dents, bent nails and injured thumbs. But in capable hands it can be used to get the job done well and fast. You want to use this strong tool after doing your homework, after involving them in discovery, after quantifying the size of the prize—to help them over the finish line.

7. Lay the foundation for agreement and action

"I've learned that people will forget what you said, people will forget what you did, but people will never forget how you made them feel."
—Maya Angelou

In this step you want to build understanding with your employees that there IS a solution, and it IS worth doing. This is a company-wide effort.

As we just explored, people need to feel safe, secure, heard, and valued before it feels okay to say, *I'M IN*. They need and deserve to be edified about the whys and hows of the project. They need to know what's ahead, what success is going to look like, and what the expectations are going to be.

You appointed a project champion to lead your discovery process, and you've gone to Gemba (where the work gets done!), so you have already established a respectful, open relationship with your employees—off to a good start!

You and your champion could try to persuade them with a lot of data and prove beyond a shadow of a doubt that this is the right thing to do. And you could also annoy them, make them feel defensive, and want to string you up by your thumbs rather than do the project (trust me, I've gotten that reaction!) Enter the emotional piece …

Here is the most effective way I've found to lay the foundation for change: ***Help people see the truth for themselves.*** Coach your champion to make the team the hero. Let the team members present—to you, to your board, to a steering committee. The best presentations we've ever been part of are ones where the client's people presented them, not us as outsiders.

Train and prepare your management teams to present the case to *their* people. You want to show instead of tell and get THEM to embrace the truth and tell the truth themselves. This approach goes a long way to making sure they feel part of the team, because they are! Seeking their input also makes them part of the design of the new process that will ensure a successful result.

Big picture upside

Over the years I have noticed an interesting thing about operations in a manufacturing company. It's the one business arena where the employees likely never went to college, have never had leadership or skill training outside their particular job, and, for many, working for this company has been their only job.

In many ways this is what helps them be an incredibly effective part of a small team that's going to generate results and make big changes. What they have to offer is gold if you know how to bring it to the light!

However, it's not typical to just go up to people on the line and say, "Hey, head to the conference room and brainstorm fifteen ideas for us to take to the marketing department." That would not be productive. Instead, tell them: "Hey, guys, you're our team. You have shared ideas with us in the past. And maybe we've been a bit thick-headed. But we believe that you can increase the output at this line—maybe you're the only ones! So, we want you to try something out. It's your job for three days, and you don't have to produce anything. Here are the tools, here's the approach we're thinking of. And on Friday we want you to report out what you came up with."

It's a beautiful thing to see a maintenance person, an operator, and a supervisor put their heads together, spend a week, and fundamentally change something that's going to impact the financial statements in a significant way!

As you take on this process, keep this "gold" in mind and make sure you tap into the ideas, talents, experience—and hearts—of ALL your people.

Wake up your team: Bottom line

➡ How do you help your people accept that the opportunities you identify are worth seeking?

⁎ Make them feel they're valued and respected by the company—and that their input matters. To be heard.

⁎ Let them hear the truth—yes, they CAN handle the truth! If they understand the purpose of the change and the data supporting it, they will be more apt to embrace the process (and the change that will follow).

⁎ Encourage trust in the CEO and management teams that the change is not a disguised ploy to get rid of them.

⁎ Help them to believe they're empowered (or about to be) to see the change through—they're in a safe problem-solving culture in which they can take ownership of their work.

➡ Six steps to tackle those Opportunity Indicators:

1. Assign a champion.
2. Get to the truth: Go to Gemba.
3. Quantify and clarify the truth.
4. Synthesize the assessment.
5. Present an irresistible business case for the proven path.
6. Lay the foundation for agreement and action.

➡ The most effective way to lay the foundation for change: Help people see the truth for themselves. The best presen tations we've ever been part of are ones where the client's people presented them, not us as outsiders.

CHAPTER NINE

The Real Prize—Preparing Your Team for Transformational Action

Now that I've gotten you all excited to make these changes, I'm going to say, *"You can't do it!"*

WELL ... ALLOW ME TO put it this way: Here is what you CAN'T do: You cannot do any kind of meaningful improvement initiative by yourself (and I know many CEOs who've tried). And why would you want to? You're a grower of leaders working together on the design and execution of a common goal toward achieving shocking profit!

This chapter focuses on how to prepare your ENTIRE COMPANY to take action, *not just for immediate results but for its own transformation.*

Help your people see the SIZE OF THE PRIZE

Even the best assessments and fancy hardbound reports won't lead to results UNLESS the team accepts the value and importance of the solutions.

You've likely heard the ages-old proverb: "If you give a man a fish, you have fed him for a day, but if you teach him to fish, you have fed him for a lifetime." Moral: Let your people FEEL the size of the prize and how instrumental they are in making it happen.

In this context, teaching your people to fish means **helping them develop their potential to take advantage of these hidden assets**—the Black Gold—that have been hiding beneath the surface of your company.

You, the CEO, are going to give a hand up, not out, to your team members. You're going to help your team take ownership over their areas. You'll teach them and they in turn will replicate it, like building compound interest on a loan.

The result? Your people just keep on building value that brings more value, and the company performs better and generates additional profit from the effort. This is what transformational change looks like, and **your life is going to be forever changed because of it!**

"It ain't over 'til it's over." Mega Machining Company made specialized machine parts at a very high margin. The company was losing money. Over the prior two years, the private equity firm was investing some $100,000 a month into the company, to the tune of $2.5 million dollars over two years. On top of that, customers were leaving due to poor service.

The PE firm finally said, *We're done; we're not putting any more money into this. We're turning it over to the lender.* The lender hired us when they "got the keys."

We started by studying the situation to hunt for hidden value and risks. On the shop floor I asked a question of two of the machine operators: "How do people know what to work on next?" They shared, "Oh, it's easy. When a job is ready to be worked on, the supervisor takes the paperwork out and puts it in the middle of the floor. When an operator finishes the job they're working on, they just come and pick up a job to work on next."

It makes sense, doesn't it? But here was the problem: *There was no monitoring, no prediction, no schedule.* How would you know if someone took 90 minutes to do a 60–minute job—or 60 minutes to do a 90–minute job? How would you know if the job was getting done well or not? How would you balance things out at the end of the day to know where you stood? I asked the supervisors these questions and they looked at me blankly with no answers. They didn't know how their operators were doing their jobs—and the operators didn't either, because there were fuzzy boundaries and no accountability!

We presented a plan that would add over $100,000 per month in profitability within twelve weeks. Without exaggeration, the company broke even in three months, and from then on increased cash flow every month, simply by changing how they had been running the operation!

The punchline: By going to where the work was done, interviewing the operators and completing our analysis, we defined the size of the prize—and it was compelling! We modeled the impact of change, and it provided the motivation to try something new.

> **The result? Operators and supervisors alike were sharing ownership of their work, and seeing how their value fit into the company's vision.**

When your people clearly understand and embrace their role:

- They know what success looks like and they're given the authority to achieve it.

- They have the dignity of taking responsibility for their role.

- They're being noticed for how they work, what their particular skills might be and the ways in which they're contributing as part of the team.

Using a football metaphor, you may have a superstar player who just wants to run fast and catch the ball. That's fine, but it's not going to work in the pros. The coach isn't going to tolerate it—not that they're trying to limit the player, but they have a whole team to look at toward the ultimate goal of winning games. If you've got a skill, they're going to build a play around your skill. Everybody knows the play on your team. They all know when it's done right and when it isn't.

The same is true in a company. On the shop floor it's not a team of eight individual ball players who don't know how to play together. Instead, they're working together to cross the goal line: to serve the customer. *We're going to do it the best way we can.* When it works it's a beautiful thing!

The same holds true for the entire company, not just for the workers on the floor. Everyone is pulling together with the process, the plays, the rules, and what they have practiced to win. As you might have guessed, this is where you, the grower of leaders, get to empower, delegate to, and train your up-and-coming stars.

So, armed with a common belief that there is a problem worth solving and/or a vision worth pursuing, **let's get to work!**

Three steps to prepare your company for action

With your assessment report in hand, your noble goal is this: *A good plan which will address a real need with key people involved in the process.*

You and your leadership team will plot the overall critical path from the current state to your designed future state. You'll decide on your high-priority initiatives, choose for each an initial application area that will yield some fast results—and craft the plan to achieve them.

Here are the steps to achieve these objectives:

1.   **Build the plan with the end in mind.**

2.   **Refine your initiative: Break down the elements.**

3.   **Pave the path to the future state: Choose your first initiatives.**

By now you're probably curious as to what your company is about to embark on, so let me give you an overview: You'll work through the initiatives according to the proven path I am outlining in this and *Chapter Ten* (about plan implementation), step by step, using ProAction's time-tested approaches and tips. Your goal will be to identify and complete some early wins—through what we call "initial applications"—designed to result in financial returns that will help fund more improvements.

Problems will get solved, hidden value will be leveraged, and each one of the recommended initiatives will unfold over time *as self-funded continuous improvements*. All this while your organization is conducting business. In doing so, your employees will embed these techniques into habits, build a problem-solving culture, and you will continually develop and nurture leaders within your company!

1. Build the plan with the end in mind.

Reverse engineering is my favorite way to describe building with the end in mind—not the typical meaning of taking someone else's product and breaking it down to see how it was made. In this case it's a planning tool I call the "Gap Plan," defined as the gap between the current state and the overall context of the future state you want to have in, say, six months, as a first phase (or could be the final solution) of the initiative.

You've defined what the end game is; now you're breaking down what you can actively pursue right now within a three- to four-month window—the milestone state.

This is not a linear exercise. A foundation of your gap plan is to notice how a change in one area will affect another area or process (within the main initiative and across each of the others). As you progress, you'll identify what I call the "building blocks," those activities that have to fit together—in the right order—to build a solid path to success.

For example, one common foundational block relates to systems. To upgrade or procure the system, setting it up and training operators takes a substantial amount of time and, often, investment. With your reverse-engineered plan, you will have assembled and scheduled the appropriate team to get started on the project early, so that when the teams are ready to implement their initiative(s), the systems to support them will already be up and running—and benefits accrue in short order!

Also, with a reverse-engineered plan, it would soon be clear whether or not the particular improvement you're working on will fit the overall plan or be an action that is irrelevant or even counterproductive.

Let me explain what you DON'T want your Gap Plan to look like...

"I did Lean!" The CEO of Imperial Transport Company called us in to consider an improvement project. Beverly emphatically and enthusiastically told me, "Here's what I want you to do. I want you to come in and work for two months and address the specific product flow issue we know we need to improve."

I respond, "Well, we could do that ... yet, if we come in and start working on one of the aspects of your business without understanding if it's actually a bottleneck or a critical path issue, then we have wasted our time and your money."

She persisted: "In one of our six plants, they found a way to do a line process that was taking 51 hours down to just 20 hours. We want to replicate that."

I agreed that's a big difference, however: "We don't yet know how that operation is going to affect the five other operations you need to complete the product. If any one of those takes 51 hours, then speeding up one part of the line doesn't help because other operations may be too slow to keep up—you would end up with the same 51-hours to finish the product. There's more to analyze here.

"Our work is to make a holistic assessment of your operations, find the root cause of unnecessary bottlenecks or waste and reveal hidden value that, together, will improve performance and profitability. If we focus on one specific area, you won't yield those results."

If you ever want to see fireworks, watch a salesperson tell a potential buyer they won't sell them what they want—it is something to see! Happily, Beverly understood the importance of evaluating the system as a whole. We had to design every operation to run at the speed of customer demand. We went on to complete a successful project together.

Stabilize before you improve. Let's define the two concepts:

"Stabilizing" means that you reach a point where you can predict a decent outcome over time. Your processes are consistent enough to forecast future actions and results. This is an example of what often happens with our clients—a situation that will need to be stabilized before any improvement steps can be taken:

On the 25th of the month, the private equity sponsor called up the CEO: "Hey, Chester, how's the month going?"

Response: "Good, we should hit our budget for the month."

Then five days later they missed it by 20 percent. So, the sponsor naturally asked Chester: *"How did that happen?"* There could be 20 different reasons—shipping delays, problems building the product, etc. The root issue is that Chester was **predicting outcomes based on an unstable system**, instead of being on top of the variables that could affect the monthly numbers. And the gap that needed to be addressed. Why? Because that same scenario would more than likely happen next month and the next, and the next, because an unstable situation couldn't be counted on. Thus, any effort at change would not stick.

"Improving" moves from one state to a better state, often an ongoing process as opposed to a one-time action. (By the way, this defines "continuous improvement," a combination of small improvements over time and huge, breakthrough, transformative ones.)

Your reverse-engineered plan allows you to determine what needs to be stabilized before you consider making improvements on any level. Baseball metaphor: You have to round all the bases in the right order to score a run!

> **The antithesis of a plan is a random act.**

This is a great illustration of what I mean by a random act of improvement:

"Now, *that's* a wrap!" Remember our delicious engagement with Willy Wonder Chocolates? We were called in to conduct diligence on their plant processes (if the Lucy and Ethel sketch at the chocolate factory comes to mind, you're right on the money[22]). There were about 30 people on the line wrapping chocolate bars and putting them into boxes. The supervisor, Warren, was walking us through the operations when he stopped and said, almost bursting with pride, "See that lady over there? That's Louise. She

wraps twice as many as anybody else. She's a superstar!" It was heart-warming to watch how respectfully he spoke of her.

As nice as this was, I wonder if you're thinking what I'm thinking (and what Warren evidently hasn't thought of): If Louise was able to wrap chocolate bars so quickly, why didn't they have everybody learn her approach, do it the way she did it, and double their entire output?

Two relevant lessons can be gleaned from this story:

1. Louise essentially created a random act of improvement, which was awesome. But the fact that she improved the process was lost on the group. It wasn't part of a sustainable change effort or planned conversion such that the other 29 people were trained to do the same thing. While her work was recognized, it was largely irrelevant as just one of 30 in terms of potential total output.

2. Warren as supervisor didn't think to take Louise's improvement to the next level. And that was understandable—another case of lack of empowerment in the job. He was a "producer" in the system, and didn't believe the process was his to improve or change. He was not "the leader" here; it may even have been beyond his imagination or what he thought was acceptable to change anyone's approach to their work.

2. Refine your initiative:
Break down the elements into individual bricks.

I often refer to transformational change in terms of the "proven path," how the accumulation of thoroughly vetted experience and analyses get us to the future state of shocking profit. Taking the metaphor further helps you visualize what this can look like as you develop your Gap Plan.

You want to identify the portions of the path between here and the future, with a milestone application or a component of a bigger solution that can be accomplished, measured, and completed. Picture these portions as bricks or blocks that are intentionally designed and arranged to pave that path.

Break things down into manageable chunks (bricks). There are different kinds of projects to solve for different conditions and needs and to guarantee the results you're seeking. Besides accomplishing these objectives, the benefits of this approach are many:

- ***You're getting obvious problems solved*** in a methodical way, revealing measurable results.

- ***Your "wins" help bolster your business case***, converting those folks who haven't yet completely seen the size of the prize.

- ***You learn who the good leaders are*** or the diamonds in the rough whose leadership skills could be developed.

- ***You fund the achievement of the steady state*** which will support the next initiative, and so on.

- *Confidence and enthusiasm are boosted around the win.* It can literally be an energy pill, particularly in a situation where the company has long been struggling, and everyone needs a boost!

Here is how we break it down, ranging from relatively simple to more complex:

- **The Mondays (Quick Win):** Low-cost, low-effort improvements that you can simply decide to do, starting on Monday. Often these come to light when cross-functional teams review an existing process. For example, when someone learns that IT is running a report that you no longer use, you simply decide to stop running that report. It is a satisfying item to check off the list and to celebrate!

> **Snow-Be-Gone Company made snowplows.** One of the reasons they brought us in was that it was taking nine months to build an order and customers were complaining. We discovered that one bottleneck was a particular part that took a couple of months to get, and our investigation revealed they used this part two or three times a month. It was very expensive, so Fred, their CFO, understandably told his people: "You cannot order this part until we have the customer order in place." So, there has been no inventory to draw from, causing a lag time for every single order!
>
> We proposed to stop waiting until they had a project to order the part for it—simple! Try buying three and when an order comes in, replace that part. They started conservatively by buying one, then every week ordered another one to build a buffer so if a customer ordered a different amount in one month, the plant could handle it in stride.

In one day and one simple call to the supplier, we reduced their lead time by two months—check! From this springboard, we could now look at other improvement initiatives to increase efficiencies and reduce the lead time even further.

- **Quick Kills:** A tactical change which requires a focused effort in one or a couple of areas to achieve an improvement, usually addressable in a short period of time or through a single resource. Sometimes these improvements can be dramatic:

  > **For example, we helped onboard a new portfolio company** for a PE firm after we had identified that they were overpaying for their raw materials and packaging. Leadership invited us to negotiate new terms on their behalf with existing suppliers. We negotiated concessions from these suppliers that exceeded their starting profitability. In the first quarter of our client's ownership of this company we literally doubled earnings (EBITDA).

- **Kaizen events:** Team-based, focused improvement events which require formal problem solving (A-3), mapping (VSM et al) and team-building tools. It typically involves cross-functional areas collaborating to achieve a targeted outcome and lasts about a week. They look for measurable and sustainable improvements and provide a review of their results and planning for follow-up actions.

  > For example, we conducted a one-week kaizen event on a manufacturing operation to rebalance the line. The team conducted a time study on every task required to complete

the operation and then redistributed them. In this case the operation employed 5 people. By redistributing the tasks to hit the takt time, they were able to match output to customer demand while freeing up 2 of the 5 people to work on other operations.

- **Highly Complex and Low-Capex Projects:** Some changes require several moving parts, approvals, and participation by multiple departments and/or companies. They may take longer to implement but do not require a large capital investment.

  The Alpha story starting each section of this book is a good example of a complex, low-capex project. To double output, the client had to move equipment, change how they scheduled the plant, started preventative maintenance, and implement problem-solving habits. While it took 4 months and had many moving parts, they did not have to buy any equipment or new systems.

- **Highly Complex and High-Capex Projects:** Complex projects that often require significant investment and detailed planning. In some cases, a company may realize that improving capacity, reliability, and velocity in their factories will enable them to satisfy demand and continue to grow with fewer facilities. This type of change will require many quick kills, kaizens, and low-capex projects, as well as extensive capital to wind down and ramp up locations.

Remember, the goal here is to fund these investments from the results of earlier improvements!

3. Pave the path to the future state: Choose your first initiatives.

We have our bucket of bricks, now we want to plot out how we're going to lay them into a path to the future state—how they will relate to each other, interact with each other, and pave the path forward in a systematic, results-driven, self-funded way.

Sticking with the building metaphor, think of this as a construction project, where the foundation (initial application area) needs to be laid before the framing can be done. The electrical grid needs to be installed before the drywall is put up, and so on. Some materials or skills needed for the building will be generic; some will be custom and need more lead time. Some activities will require specialized skills (subject matter or tech experts, for example) to be brought in for support.

Make these considerations in terms of *speed, complexity and relative impact of implementation*:

- **Factor in its impact.** Consider how effective the impact could be and how fast it could be accomplished, preferably with the resources at hand.

- **Tie the application to the financials.** Consult your assessment report and work those numbers. You get to prove the point and play it out in real time.

- **What is the "worst" problem?** Often there is a situation that is consistently happening in a department, factory, line, etc., of which you are (and everyone else is) aware. Sometimes this is where the biggest opportunity lies. It may surprise you when I say that we routinely choose the "worst" plant to start with, because, as they say, there's no place to go but up. We get quick wins right away and have regularly taken those plants all the way to the top of the list of best performing!

- *Choose the problem that involves the most energized team*, thus, the highest chance of a successful resolution. Or consider which leaders are already receptive to the initiative so they can lead the pack with a big success.

- *Recognize the bricks that are required for stability.* Remember that certain areas will need to be stabilized before improvement is possible or prudent.

- *All in or a test drive?* Decide if you want to roll out an approach for the whole company at once or do it in one department, then go on to another one. One is time-based, the other is location-based.

- *Consider the speed and complexity of implementing.* You may choose bricks that will likely not be strategic in their impact but will provide relief.

A time-tested approach to evaluate the ease of implementing relative to its impact is the *rack-and-stack* methodology, allowing you to assess and organize the steps you're reverse engineering for the initiative. Rack-and-stack is typically an IT term—in this application it means to prioritize the changes, one brick building upon another, which together will demonstrate results. Rank the steps based on specific criteria, always reflecting their relative importance, impact or value to the initiative.

Then choose the initial quick-win initiatives that will kick off the process and initiate the self-funding cycle.

Anything outside the plan is irrelevant. In this plan, there are no random acts of improvement! This is how to keep your eye on the prize—by designing a focused plan to take you forward without distractions or wasted time and money.

Consider process, systems, and technology, in many ways the foundations of a company's success. You may notice that we focus on process changes in this book. Here's why: Changes to systems and technology are complicated and expensive. They add overhead and cost. Process changes allow us to test the true capacity of our systems and technology, and to squeeze more juice out of those oranges!

Also, process changes tie directly into behavior, leadership development, problem solving, and culture—addressing processes changes behavior, changing behavior changes culture. We find that companies are well served to get their day-to-day processes and habits aligned and effective, because they will generate profits, capital, a problem-solving culture, and experience in continuous improvement. And tight processes will lead to effective utilization of new systems and technology. It's a beautiful cycle.

Something my partner and friend, Doug, shared with me many times: "Catch the ball before you run with it!"

Big picture upside

When you "see the prize," everything changes. The grind has purpose. The team has direction. And decisions—big and small—start aligning with long-term value, not just short-term fires. The upside of this mindset isn't just more profit (though that's a nice bonus). It's momentum.

Now is the moment to help your team see what you see—a problem-solving culture that can do things better, improve and scale faster, and become far more valuable (not only to a buyer but to everyone in the company). You've done the work to become a developer of leaders—now's the time to activate that investment. Don't just hand out answers—teach them how to think, how to lead, how to fish.

Help your people connect the dots between their daily roles and the company's larger mission. Give them the tools to move from reactive to proactive. That's how real change takes root. That's how culture scales. And that's how *you* get to step forward with confidence into the next chapter—implementation—with a team that's not just aligned but lined up at the gate ready to run!

The real prize: Bottom line

⇨ Give a hand up, not out, to your team members, help them take ownership over their areas. You'll teach them and they in turn will replicate it, like building compound interest on a loan. This leads to transformational change, and your life is going to be forever changed because of it!

⇨ Break down your initiative criteria into the "building blocks" that will pave the way to the future state you desire. Then get the first one rolling, looking toward quick wins. A goal of this approach is to succeed with the short-term low-hanging fruit that will fund the next stages (if not the rest of the project).

⇨ Three steps to prepare your company for action:

　✳ Build the plan with the end in mind.
　✳ Refine your initiative: Break down the elements.
　✳ Pave the path to the future state: Choose your first initiatives.

Shocking Success

"Action is about making sustainable change to realize shocking profit. Yet the real value comes in using the need to change to create a problem-solving culture and a leader development machine. You are now in the business of producing leaders."
—Timothy Van Mieghem

IN SECTION II WE MADE the preparations to turn that hidden value you have found into a strategic plan for improvement, profit, and growth (financially and personally as a leader of developing leaders).

In Section III we'll explore how to take action that not only soothes symptoms and solves real problems but also creates a ***self-improving organization—to elevate your team into a group of problem-solvers, proud owners of the excellent work they do, and leaders in their own right!***

Now we're all about ACTION. So much thought, planning, and hard work have brought you and your team to this point. You know you have worthy goals and plans. Now it's time to implement them!

Chapter Ten is about executing your improvement plan. *How will you lead this collection of initiatives to reach your company's successful* *future state?* Through the proven path of problem-solving methodology, you'll take your team through the change cycles of self-funded incremental improvements which will collectively develop into a problem-solving, continuous-improvement, profit-making culture.

Chapter Eleven is about the Virtual Cycle of sustaining, scaling, and enjoying ethical profit. *How do you WANT to take your company to its next level of growth?* You sustain your standardized process to guide continuous improvement going forward with a strong team and problem-solving culture. The result? A workplace of happy employees who find meaning and satisfaction in their work and a company that thrives in predictable growth and scaling. And you create a position that opens up exciting opportunities and frees you up to explore your personal future!

Action

Scene 3: The Transformation. Action.

ProAction and the Alpha team mapped out the process and applied Lean manufacturing, demand planning, and scheduling processes. Together they reduced downtime by 80%, improved first pass yield from 90% to 95%, re-laid out the plant, and developed and implemented standard work. That was the easy part.

Bob, the CEO coached Kevin (the plant manager), "Kevin, you need to unlearn old habits and become comfortable holding the team accountable to follow the new approach. Stop solving problems yourself and begin to truly lead."

Kevin, replied, "I understand, Bob. I'll do my best to lead the team."

And he did. Over a few short months, the team developed new skills and took on the new authority to solve problems.

Scene 4: The Victory

By the end of April, the plant produced 99,000 units, eliminating the backlog and setting up to produce 100,000 units each month *without* new labor or equipment. The cost per unit dropped from $7.50 to $3.70. Annual earnings increased by more than $2.9 million. The sales team won back hundreds of store locations that had been lost in prior years. Within three months scrap was cut in half and continued to improve as Bob fostered a climate of trust and innovation.

Everyone was engaged in finding and solving problems.

"We've done it, Kevin," said Bob. "The transformation was remarkable. The most important change is the new culture. We've created a safe atmosphere where people feel free to experiment and learn."

And Kevin replied, "I can finally think, go home, and have dinner with my family."

~ THE (Shockingly Profitable) END ... NOT!

This marks the **beginning** of Kevin creating leaders, relying on stable processes and nurturing a problem-solving culture. Just imagine what is next!

CHAPTER TEN

Execution—Rubber, Meet Road!

THE PROVEN PATH HAS BEEN laid so you can see how each brick interrelates and takes you forward. Now you're setting the mortar—the time has come to execute your improvement plan in a way that delivers results as you go, develops leaders, and leads to sustainable, even transformational change.

Let's recap. You have:

- Quantified the size of the prize.

- Built your business case and brought along your people to lay the foundation for change management.

- Formed a plan with the end in mind, prioritized the initiatives, and prepared a timeline for proceeding.

- Pulled forward your Mondays, Quick Kills, and Kaizen events that will see results, build momentum, and initiate the self-funding cycle.

You're now implementing the strategic approach that will direct all your improvements to a future state; stay focused with no waste or random acts; pay for themselves because every single project has an ROI; and with this foundation, build momentum that just keeps feeding itself forward to continuous improvement and predictable, sustained, not-so-shocking profit.

Enough talk! Enough with the suspense! You're probably giddy with the same anticipation Jed Clampett felt the first time he floated in his cement pond; you're waiting for me to reveal the *silver-bullet signature foolproof solution* that will guarantee a perfect implementation of your improvement plan.

Well ... it is true that each of us at The ProAction Group is passionate about finding the best ways to apply our proven principles in the real worlds of our clients. Yet, in over 25 years of trial-and-error learning, we're not prescribing a new methodology, nor do I have any new acronyms for you—sorry, not sorry!

You and I are going to explore the basics of executing a plan well, and cover tips and lessons taken from the ProAction experience, starting with reliance on our particularly successful applications of two classic tools:

- **Plan, Do, Check, Act (PDCA)**, the four-stage model for continuous improvement in business developed by pioneering statistician, professor, and consultant Dr. Edward Deming.[23]

- **A-3 Problem Solving methodology**, a Toyota-originated practice of problem-solving which forms the cornerstone of Lean management practices[24].

These tools lay the proven path developed over 60 years ago. I'd say Toyota is the living meme for continuous improvement—and it's hard to argue with their performance, so why reinvent the wheel?

The difference here is that you'll see exactly how these tools work in organizations like yours. One of the beauties of these classic, elegant methodologies is that they apply whether your team is assigned to a Monday, a Quick Kills, a Kaizen, or complex PDCA and problem-solving cycles!

The building blocks of improvement plans: Plan, Do, Check, Act (PDCA)

When we support a client in driving change, we rely on this simple yet powerful methodology. It works, and we have never found a shortcut. Here are descriptions and applications of the four components of PDCA as we deploy them:

1. PLAN

Planning in the execution phase takes you from the 50,000-foot view down to the 500-foot view, and involves three important steps:

1. ***Define the problem you're addressing in this improvement initiative.*** Gold to be mined: *Invest time in this area!* We humans tend to like to jump right into solving a problem, but we often find out that our group has vague agreement and different conceptions for what we're actually trying to solve. It can feel like we're making progress until things are brought to an abrupt halt when someone raises an objection that could have been addressed earlier—had the problem been defined more effectively.

    > *"If I had an hour to save the world from impending doom,*
    > *I would spend 55 minutes studying the problem and*
    > *five minutes on the solution."*
    > —Attributed to Dr. Albert Einstein

This phase typically includes writing down everything that is true and relevant to the situation. No judgment involved and just the facts. You're stating what is currently happening that impacts your performance. Completing this process tends to reduce emotions around the topic and paves the way to developing a shared and granular vision.

2. **Develop the metrics and data points** you will collect in the DO phase to monitor the change and its impact. *How will you measure progress and results?*

3. **Predict and set targets.** Not only will this help you evaluate the effectiveness of the changes and how well you followed the plan, it will also develop the critical skill of forecasting, which informs decision making and efficient resource management to minimize waste and lower costs (as we discussed in Section I).

2. DO

This is the action phase. Finally, after all the visioning, mapping, interviewing, observing, and collaborating, you make the change! You execute the plan and collect the data.

For a Monday project, the DO portion can take minutes. For most Kaizen projects, the DO portion takes one to three days of active work buffered by the upfront planning and training and back-end of collecting the data.

3. CHECK

After implementing the plan, you leverage the data you have been and are still collecting to evaluate the results against your initial objective. Focus on identifying any deviations to the plan, how the actual results compare to what you predicted, and determine the reasons for those deviations.

Throughout this book we have talked about the value of predicting an outcome, tracking the actual results, deploying countermeasures during the game to get to the goal, and then studying the results. This is the same activity.

4. ACT

In this final stage you take appropriate action to address any deviations, discrepancies, or deficiencies found in the CHECK phase. Often, the conclusion of this ACT phase reveals that you're not yet able to predict a consistently good outcome. If this is the case, you "rinse and repeat"— start another PDCA cycle!

If you determine that you have a standardized process that is followed by all and achieves your vision, then you're done! Ready for the next initiative (after you celebrate, of course).

Be prepared: The first time you lead your group through a PDCA cycle may feel like pulling teeth. People will resist, stumble, learn, scrape their knees, and eventually work their way through to the solution. By the second or third time, they will develop their sea legs, buoyed by the results they're experiencing. You'll notice who the natural leaders are whom you can support and develop. Then you reach the sweet spot: After five or six cycles, you won't be able to stop them from doing it! It will have become second nature, like breathing, to your people. They move forward together like an efficient, well-oiled machine, taking on initiatives large and small.

> **This collection of initiatives becomes continuous improvement, and a problem-solving culture becomes embedded in the organization.**

Everyone is participating in helping the company along the maturity path. THIS is how you add a million dollars to the EBITDA and keep finding another million or more every single year. It's the difference between adding a million dollars to the bottom line and a process that does it every year. One is an event, and one is a process. We want the process, through a problem-solving culture.

Problem-solving methodology for lasting change initiatives

We welcome headwinds. We want challenges. We want to address and confront problems as they arise, rather than checking off boxes, moving on, and sweeping issues under the rug that will certainly trip us up later.

In my experience, a problem-solving methodology and culture is the ONLY way to go. Consider the cultural contrast between companies like Toyota and several of the American manufacturers. For example, I've heard that at an American company, reporting a quality issue on the assembly line could lead to severe repercussions—imagine having your tire slashed because someone feared missing a bonus. In stark contrast, Toyota empowers every employee, on every level including janitorial, to pull a cord on the production line to halt operations if they spot a problem. This practice not only ensures safety and quality but also fosters a culture where problems are openly addressed and resolved.

> *"In most organizations, problems are not viewed as opportunities for improvement, but as failures, and thus are hidden rather than addressed."* [25]
> —Brian Tracy

Here is the mindset you want to embrace: When your plan encounters unexpected challenges or when a team member raises a concern, you need a clear, structured methodology to break down the issue, analyze it, and adapt your approach. By getting good at addressing these problems, **you create an environment of continuous improvement—one where every obstacle becomes an opportunity to learn and evolve!**

As you can see, the PDCA cycle is built on problem-solving steps, techniques, and attitudes, particularly in the PLAN and CHECK phases. There are a number of methodologies available that lead a team through effective problem solving.

In ProAction's experience, combining rigorous problem-solving approaches, tools, and training within the PDCA framework is a proven path that helps build that problem-solving culture. We tend to use the A3 Problem-Solving methodology[26] which Toyota developed to build onto the PDCA Cycle. We leverage our problem-solving training and execution to:

- *Clearly define the problem* and its impact on the organization.

- *Use data to analyze the root cause* of the problem.

- *Develop solutions that address the root cause*, then outline an action plan.

- *Implement the plan* and monitor its effectiveness.

- *Evaluate the results and standardize* successful practices, or revise the plan as needed.

Here are some key insights and tips for effective problem solving that we have learned (the hard way!) over the years. I'm sharing them here to help smooth your own proven path:

Problem solving is at the root of claiming and creating value. Do not be afraid to invest in subject matter experts, hired guns, and eager recruits who can accelerate your learning curve and get it done!

Separating the people from the problem is the best way to get to the root of a problem. Sounds counterintuitive, doesn't it? Well, we humans tend to be brutal on problems and graceful with people. When you address the problem itself, you want to take out of the solution equation all the perceptions, agendas, emotions, hesitations, and the rest. Gaining clarity on this idea is just the start. It's a process that will take a little time, so give yourself and your team some grace as they begin to trust the safety you're creating and nurturing. Everyone needs to believe it in their head and in their gut. Be patient—but insistent—with your team on learning and practicing this mindset.

Surfacing problems is to be encouraged, supported and even celebrated. It may sound crazy, yet raising it up, airing it, and examining it is how everyone can come together at the root level and solve the problem for good!

The real power comes in solving problems in relationship with the team. It's my personal preference to solve problems on my own;

however, this is something I have witnessed repeatedly, and now I'm a fan! The more you share, the more vulnerable you become, and the more your team will trust this new problem-solving culture. And I guarantee you will be surprised by the innovative solutions and supportive energy that pop out of your team. Resist holding people back.

Think of it this way: Solving a problem on your own creates a thread that pulls you toward your envisioned goal via one thin strand. Solving problems together creates multiple threads that are woven together, stronger and faster. That is how you move mountains!

The kickoff

You are ready. You have your plan and approach built on clarity, awareness, and acceptance by your leadership team and key stakeholders.

I have enjoyed promising that you as the CEO don't get to solve the problems or drive the process. But don't feel left out—and don't take off just yet for that extended tropical cruise you've thought you could plan. You HAVE a critical role, and here is how you stack the deck: Empower your team to take relevant action, become leaders, and learn how to grow new leaders themselves!

A common question I get from audiences when I speak is: "Why do projects fail?" It is a fun question because the answer often surprises them (and makes some people squirm when they recognize themselves). You may not want to hear it, but the answer is rarely—never—that we were wrong on the idea, the data, or the principles, or that there was anything wrong with the team. **The CEO was the roadblock.** Failure comes when the CEO takes a passive role. Projects fail when the CEO doesn't show up for the project or their team.

The successful CEO doesn't necessarily demand obedience, but they require participation from the team. The successful CEO doesn't micromanage the process; they encourage people to participate and give it their best shot.

"Loyalty has its price." We coached a team on putting their spend and sourcing out to bid, even though they'd worked with many of their suppliers for decades—they knew a lot of these people very well, and some kept putting out all these reasons why *we can't switch! We can't switch!* Familiarity bred excuses for not vetting these sources.

The toughest one to convince was the CEO, Sabrina. Her best friend, Evelyn, owned the supplier company, their kids were in each other's weddings …. Geez! We repeatedly stressed to her that this process was simply about gathering information and making informed decisions, not about the relationships involved.

In the end, our analysis showed that this supplier was costing the company $500,000 a year, while a highly qualified alternative could do the work for $400,000. The CEO went to her friend to ask about the discrepancy, and Evelyn responded: "Oh, I can understand that. They're a much larger company. They have their own internal maintenance; they can do it themselves." Various excuses but no clear data was offered. Sabrina listened to it all, and said: "You know, I love you, but I'm not writing you an extra $100,000 check for the same work." With the CEO's blessing the company switched to the other supplier, who worked out well.

I am not advocating for the CEO to simply pick a side, or about blind compliance. It's about requiring a thorough process where every decision is justified on its merits. If a proposal is vetoed, the CEO should ask why and hold the team accountable. Success is dependent upon active participation and responsible decision-making at every level.

1. Assign the team.

One of your roles is to select the team(s) to implement the initiative. These are the positions to fill:

Sponsor: Executive providing the authority to do the project—this would be you.

Champion: Leader ultimately responsible to deliver the project. Here are the attributes we find relevant to look for in the selection of the champion.

- ***Responsibility and accountability*** for significant portions of the scope you're addressing. You want someone invested in the outcome.

- ***Ability to hold people accountable.*** This doesn't mean they relish telling people what to do. It means they're willing to impel people to succeed in their job or task, rather than do it for them or accept mediocre results.

- ***Belief in the path.*** It starts with trust in you and trust in the proven path, but doesn't mean they will support everything the whole time without question. Some of the best leaders would not buy a new approach from some slick consultant from Chicago (believe me, I know *...*). *They would have to see it to believe it. And when they see the data and the evidence, they start to change.*

- ***NOT overly invested in*** how things *used to be* done.

- *Energy and enthusiasm.* As you know, I love finding diamonds in the rough. Sometimes you will pick a project champion based on leadership qualities they demonstrate, even though they have never had a supervisory position. Keep your eyes and ears open. Start by giving them a chance to lead some Mondays and Quick Kills as steps toward earning their spurs for bigger assignments.

Team members: The people who will directly work on the improvement. Each team should be:

- Cross functional (include people from operations, sales, finance, and leadership)

- Cross skills (planners, doers, galvanizers, supporters, subject matter experts)

- Cross level (leaders, managers, supervisors, and operators)

Steering Committee: Overseers of the combined group of improvements that make up your full plan. Typically, there is no need to have a separate committee for each project, Kaizen or Quick Kill endeavor. You will likely lead the steering committee, and consider including:

- CFO/Controller: While each team might have a representative from the finance and accounting group, it is important to include a financial perspective at the steering committee level. Getting the numbers right and truly understanding the full impact of the transformation is worth the effort.

- Board member: Include an outside board member when you can. Preferably someone with relevant industry or functional experience, and who will understand both the near-term tactical goals and the impact on the company of nurturing a problem-solving culture. Choose someone who can bring experience from outside the organization.

- Subject matter expert: Consider bringing in someone with deep experience in the change process you're leading—a mentor, coach, or consultant. Many of the changes your team will consider and make will seem counterintuitive. External perspectives help people get over that hump!

Stakeholders: Consider the people on the team as the representatives of the people in the company and each department. With that in mind, you're grateful to the team for taking on the work, and you also want to keep the rest of the people in the company informed on the progress, as they will be impacted by the changes. Don't forget the stakeholders!

2. Clarify the plan, then go public.

With the team selected you're now ready to kick off the process publicly. At this point, *you have one job: to lend your will, your authority, your energy, and your support to the team.* Let the champion, the team members, and the stakeholders know that their voices are important. Their participation is required, but your views and decisions are your own. Bring your brain, your voice, and your heart. Stay connected and give the team a good launch!

At the kickoff event, your presence will send a clear message to the rest of the organization. After you lend your voice to the team and the initiatives, hand the content to the project champion and leaders. These are the elements we typically recommend for a successful kickoff event:

Project plan. Review the plans developed in Chapters Eight and Nine. Give people some context on why the company is doing what it is doing in this particular order:

- The vision. *Why are we doing this? What does the future state look like?*

- How the order of improvements is set to provide stability, demonstrate early wins, fund the rest of the project, develop your young leaders, and give your teams experience in problem solving.

- Cover any acute issues or topics that might be known to the whole company. Highlight goals related to both stability and improvement. All presenters should practice transparency.

  - » Stability is achieved when you can predict a good outcome consistently. It is critical to have a process that is followed by all.
  - » Once you have a stable and solid foundation you can focus on improvements. Remember, improvements only matter when they're made in the context of the process, and impact all who carry out that role or task.

- Outline the project timeline and who is responsible for each section, project, and/or area.

Financial statements. I find this an interesting subject. Many companies are reluctant to share financial information with their team and workers. At its very core, this mindset is not compatible with a problem-solving culture. I understand there are other factors at play which may prevent you from sharing the income statement and balance sheet with the larger group. However, if you find yourself bristling at this idea, reflect on what may be the real issue: *Are you concerned that workers would know how profitable the company is?*

Is this an ego issue? If the answer is yes, I kindly recommend that if you do not want to share the financial impact of the improvements, get in touch with your support group and discuss this.

Feedback. The workers directly involved in the team will have a good vehicle for expressing their views. For other stakeholders, be sure to set up a safe way for them to provide feedback. The interviews conducted as part of building the business case would give you a good start! While people should normally follow the chain of command, it will be good for people to know they can come to you as well. Most often you will send them in turn to the person accountable for the issue or question they raise; however, an open-door policy is important (especially in the case where the person to whom they report is the problem).

3. Do weekly reviews.

After the kickoff, your main interaction with the active teams will be the weekly update, especially at the beginning of projects. There are so many moving parts and spinning plates, smaller projects that get accomplished quickly, and the additional input that people offer as they realize their world is changing. Checking in weekly helps keep forward motion, everyone on track, and the ability to head off minor issues before they morph into nastier ones.

The good news is that the structure for the weekly update is simple. Each team should cover the following:

1. What did they plan to accomplish this week?

2. What did they accomplish?

3. How do each of the metrics, leading and lagging, look this week?

4. What issues came up, if any, that will change the scope, timing, outcome, or resources of the project. And what is their plan to address those issues?

5. What is the plan for next week?

6. Adjourn!

Our ProAction team uses a Weekly Update tool (found in the *Go Deeper Appendix*), which we have honed over the years to be clear, simple, and direct. It's used on our projects with clients to monitor progress on complex projects. Essentially, it accomplishes the following:

1. Shares what the team accomplished in the prior week

2. Shares what the team will do/complete next week

3. Displays the data collected and related metrics

4. Identifies any issues that would impact the scope or effectiveness of the project.

Sustaining success on your initiatives

Consider all the foundational work described throughout this book that you have already done:

- Heard your teams' input as you investigated hidden value and risk

- Developed the business case

- Included key stakeholders in developing the solutions

- Generously shared your authority and resources throughout the company to implement the plans

After celebrating all that has been accomplished, you might be surprised (blindsided?) when you learn that, for all this hard work, **the changes don't automatically stick!**

What kills sustainability? When we do see companies returning to how they did things in the past, we often find one or more of the following culprits:

1. The leaders stopped asking questions or walking the floor.

2. No metrics were kept up that show results (lagging metrics).

3. No metrics were kept that highlight behavior (leading metrics).

4. Harshness anywhere in the ranks. People began to feel unsafe again, falling back into the old habits of hiding problems and acting defensively to protect their job.

Recidivism, or a relapse to prior behaviors, is a dangerous concept. While this process is designed to minimize any danger of people going back to the old ways, here are some additional steps you can take:

- **Be curious and nurturing.** Your role is to stay curious and involved yet refrain from solving the problems yourself. Attend the weekly meetings, go on daily Gemba walks, ask questions during tours, celebrate wins. Be sure to water this plant now that the seedlings are beginning to poke through the ground.

- **Be graceful when you need to be direct.** There are two extremes to avoid. One extreme is to simply accept whatever change people make and celebrate their effort regardless of the outcome or the alignment with the project charter and vision. The other extreme is bringing down the hammer too hard—yelling at people when they make a mistake or stray. I am sure you would vote for the middle ground: Address the situation, call them out, but do so in a way that continues to make them part of the solution. Ask questions, give them a chance to see the error, and encourage them to offer options.

- *Follow through, follow up, course correct: "The Tail"* – test for recidivism (probably longer than you think you have to), gradually scaling back monitoring until the team and company have fully embedded the problem-solving culture.

For our client projects, we've completed metrics, implementation, tracking production, and personally trained the team (over a four- to six-week period to get into the habit of actively managing daily production. "The Tail" is when we say to the client, "This is where we leave you for two weeks, then we'll be back to see how everyone is doing." *Every* time, when we return, there is some situation—or several—where people have reverted to some old habits in some shape or form. And the results are measurable: slipped production, increased waste, deliver deadlines missed, salespeople run amok on pricing/discounts, or similar.

So, we help them correct course and come back every couple of weeks to check in and correct course again. Once this works, we come back every month and sometimes every quarter before we feel we can finally say this project is complete. The team has embedded these habits until (as you now know) they cannot NOT do it the new and improved way.

We have gone back to some companies five years later, and they're still doing immensely better than before they engaged us—and they say, "Hey, thank you." Then there are those companies we see five or ten years later, and it's as if we'd never been there. Most often, it is not because the situation has materially changed; it's a slacking-off of leadership and oversight.

When a subject matter expert or accountability partner of some kind is invited in to support implementation, be sure to schedule audits, coaching and mentoring after the solutions and changes are implemented. Provide the opportunity to identify any deviations or movement back to the old ways, and correct course immediately. Keep up the monitoring, measures and metrics!

Change is hard, as we know, and even after the change is made, we often go through the motions until we start to understand and get comfortable with it. It takes time, but it DOES work!

We call the role of CEOs in these situations the "CRO," or Chief Reminding Officer ☺!

Big picture upside

In many ways this improvement effort is going to be like sitting on a rollercoaster. You bought the ticket—enjoy the ride! There will be days when it seems like you're back to square one, and times when you will feel on top of the world, invincible!

People ask me how often projects fail or go sideways—here is the reality as I see it. The ideas and changes we're pursuing and applying are all part of the proven path—it is not an experiment. This is not an attempt to *prove* that designing quality is better than inspection. To *prove* that eliminating waste is a good idea. To *prove* that we should charge customers what they're willing to pay. Or *prove* that we should put first things first (like A Customers) and second things second.

The point is: It WILL work. The concepts I've been talking about are the proven path. This book is all about helping companies apply principles that the giants like Toyota, Danaher, and Emerson Electric had developed and have proven to be successful, as well as hundreds of our client companies.

Sometimes your role as the leader and visionary will be to buoy up the team's confidence when they hit a speed bump. They will despair when a team member refuses to participate. They will hesitate when they need to let someone go who doesn't fit in the new world. Your team will be exercising new muscles. You get to help them see it through.

Of course the other reality of transformational change I get to see in my work is the incredible feeling of a major success or breakthrough—there's nothing more satisfying!

I am so excited for the final chapter where we pull it all together. Next up on this interesting journey...

Execution—Rubber, meet road: Bottom line

➡ Apply the classic tools, PDCA, and the A-3 Problem Solving methodology to implement your strategic approach to execute your change initiatives. Assign your team—sponsor, champion, cross-functional team members, steering committee, key stakeholders. Your critical role is to empower your team to take relevant action, to become leaders, and to learn how to grow new leaders!

➡ The PDCA cycles begin to become second nature, and your team begins to move forward like an efficient, well-oiled machine, taking on initiatives large and small. This collection of initiatives becomes continuous improvement, and a problem-solving culture soon gets embedded in the organization's culture.

➡ Keep on top of your processes and people. Do weekly/regular reviews; ensure metrics and measures are continued; stay curious and involved—ask questions, offer resources and support, and celebrate wins with your people, as THEY take on their roles as implementers and problem-solvers. It could be a rollercoaster ride—but it's worth it!

CHAPTER ELEVEN

How do You Sustain—Nirvana and the Virtuous Cycle!!

"Many of us trade time with our family and
loved ones to work on a business that will not survive us."
—Kim-Adele Randall,
Authentic Achievements:
The Future of Leadership, Technology and
Guaranteed Business Growth

Welcome to the end ... well, the beginning!

I SPEND A FAIR AMOUNT of time with entrepreneurs and business owners who've been running a business for upwards of 30 years. One of my first questions to them is: ***"When was the last time you took a vacation?"*** The typical response is *"Why does that matter?"* Or they just look back at me and laugh at the absurdity of the idea!

Their reaction tells me a lot about how they run their company. I tend to respond like this: "Can you imagine yourself in a situation where your people know what to do and you know that they can do it well—and you're able to go spend a month somewhere on a family vacation, talking to customers, playing softball, or thinking about your life and what's next for your business?"

A BIG pause and a dreamy look appears on their faces ... and the truth begins to dawn on them:

> **The business becomes more valuable the less it is dependent on you.**

This is good news (albeit counterintuitive)!

Let me take you down memory lane for a moment, through the stages, or maturation, of your business growth. For a visual of what this looks like, refer to my friend Tom Frey's excellent business maturity chart in the *Go Deeper Appendix* (shared with permission from Tom Frey).

It all starts with the seed stage, where you literally take an idea and create something out of nothing. You're personally doing everything: think Bill Gates and Paul Allen starting Microsoft in their garage or Sarah Blakely being her own "butt model" (her words) for Spanx. You're selling it, you're making it, you're marketing it—the whole thing. *That's a startup.*

Then a few people buy your product or service a few times. You build some volume over time until you reach a point where you literally can't do it all (with no more family members to tap for help). So, you hire some people.

You enter the next stage of growth, an ***entrepreneurial company*** where you're developing a basic organization. You begin to bring on people who are managing the product, shipping, or taking orders. You're still directing everything, and you're likely still responsible for all sales as the sole face of the company. You're the only person who knows how everything works. If you're absent from the business for any length of time (even a day), it's going to shut down or close to it. You're a CEO who is anchored in the operations of the company, needing to be present in order for things to run smoothly and profitably.

The third stage is the ***middle-market company***. You employ between 100 to 2,000 people, balancing established operational processes with an eye to growth opportunities. You as CEO are still deeply involved in both day-to-day decisions and strategic planning, ensuring accountability and keeping a close connection to the business's evolving needs.

It is likely that your company is somewhere between entrepreneurial and middle-market stage right now. What I am going to show you in this chapter is how you can use the tools, techniques, and lessons in this book to transition into a mature company.

Picture what it would look like to have more of your time freed up. Everyone in your company is no longer dependent upon you in order to do their job. You have the right systems and people in place to run the company—and make Shocking Profit! What would this mean to you? What is the difference it could make in your life? Space opens up to create options for your company, and perhaps more importantly, for yourself because ...

Freedom is the opportunity to choose the good.

The "good" means: *I love what I'm doing. I want to be present for my parents as they go through their end-of-life experience. I want to acquire a new company. If I want to go play golf or be with my grand-*

children, I can do so. You can make those choices, and your business will continue to prosper and grow.

What PE firms know that you need to know about scaling

A good Private Equity firm (meaning those who are actually interested in helping their companies evolve, not just in making fast money) leads middle-market, privately-held entrepreneurial companies into stable, sturdy, and scaling organizations.

In the best cases, they help the company build the systems, push decision-making down the line and institutionalize systems so that *the very existence of the company is no longer dependent upon any one leader.* With these advances, the PE firm can double the size of the business in a year and the company can absorb it.

You can use these same tools for your business.

For a company to reach this level, the CEO will make the transition from "chief producer" to "developer of leaders," as we talked about in Chapter Seven. Why is this important? It relieves the load the CEO has been carrying—like Atlas bearing the earth on his shoulders—and in so doing, takes the risk out of the company's value. Simply put, what happens to the company if something happens to the CEO? (This is one of the first questions a PE firm will ask when evaluating a company's value.)

What does this look like for you and your business? The answer: You let your people excel at their work, while keeping your finger on the pulse of the company and stepping into leadership when needed.

"Leadership lessons from Captain Ramius." In the 1990 spy thriller, "The Hunt for Red October,"[27] the most advanced nuclear submarine in the Russian fleet (the *Red October*) had a stellar crew that was a tight-knit group. They knew their roles, what was expected of them and the processes to be followed.

Submarine commander Captain Marko Ramius (played by Sir Sean Connery) moved all duties to members of his crew—he only issued orders to his Number 2 who would then issue the command to the appropriate crew member. A beautiful thing to witness in terms of delegation! But Capt. Ramius was always engaged. He watched on the bridge, met with his crew, and never took his eyes off the conditions and the mission.

At a crucial, life-or-death point in the story, the crew lacked the resolve to take a dangerous, unseemly action to save the ship. Capt. Ramius immediately stepped into his leadership role, saw the right action to take and had the courage to take the risks. He saved the ship. What a leader!

> **You have a fundamental choice to make, as you consider how to implement the value-creation ideas we have explored in this book and take your company to the next level of sustainable growth.**

Path #1: You can continue to drive efforts personally and rigorously, putting improvements into place. Things will change fast and drive immediate results. However, change will be short-lived. The projects will represent a set of isolated incidents rather than standard operating procedure for the entire company (mainly because it will become impossible for you to manage them all). You might get busy with other tasks and involvements. Your people will go back to their old ways, status quo, and silo thinking. In 18–24 months, one of your major A Customers will abandon ship for a competitor, and you'll be back to square one, bearing the weight of the company on your shoulders.

Path #2: You can take on real transformation, helping your company grow from an entrepreneurial company into a sturdy, stable, mature company positioned for ever greater things. One that provides a foundation for your people to develop their own leadership capabilities and those of their teams. Your people will have the chance to learn, grow, and own their successes, breaking the chain that keeps you tied to day-to-day operations. Your company will generate profits with you, without you, and beyond your capability (in the best possible way).

You can guess which path gets my vote!

A company can expect to mine its full value, even Shocking Profit, when it shifts from:

- Owner as Chief Producer to the Developer of Leaders, who share the work and lower the risk.

- Experimentation to a stable foundation with systems that maximize productivity, efficiency, and consistent customer service.

- Stress on a regular basis to a problem-solving culture which engages everyone to contribute from their own expertise, talents, and innovative ideas.

- Month-end surprises to predicted performance, leveraging vendor contracts, procurement, and sales which result in happy employees and happy customers.

All combine to dramatically increase the value of your company. For you, for your employees, for your customers—for future owners.

And here is the exciting part! You can achieve this by taking many small steps *that fund themselves*. In Chapters Nine and Ten we explored how to quilt together an action plan that demonstrates results early. This leads to the final design, the future state, the framework for continuous improvement by embedding those habits that will form your problem-solving culture.

Leveraging the PDCA cycle, over and over, is the proven path. At this execution stage of our work with clients, we often share with them that if they don't see financial impact in month two, we are doing something wrong!

Think bigger and do it right

Another benefit a PE firm brings to a company at this stage is *perspective and vision,* because they have vast experience in seeing an organization with a birds'-eye view of potential for major growth and profitability. They think big and have the luxury of flying above the brush fire. They know from experience and third-party perspective that you have choices in front of you.

> **"Looking Beyond Your Norm."** We were doing diligence on ACME Tools, a $18-million company that made molds used in manufacturing processes. They told us they were tight on capacity. We saw that they had seven machines and only six were running. We asked, "What's the story with this piece of equipment?" "Well, it's hard to find people to run it. They don't want to work for $15 an hour," was their response.

We showed our numbers to them and the PE firm and said: "If you run every line all the time, it would add $1.5 million in profit. Is the problem that people who will work for $15 an hour just don't exist, or is there something else you could do to staff these lines? What if you paid $50 an hour?" "No, we can't afford that, with the turnover we have, recruiting and training, and yada yada ..."

This was a CEO used to doing things a certain way and who hadn't looked beyond their "norm" to see what else could be possible. The Black Gold was, hiding in plain sight in the form of a perfectly serviceable, yet idle, machine. We ran more numbers by them: "If you spent $200,000 on hiring good people and keeping them, you could make another $1.5 million in earnings. That's a pretty good return any day of the week. Which would you choose, saving $200K or making $1.5 million?"

The PE firm stepped in: "You told us you could just add new equipment. That's a half-million dollars right there, and you'll need an engineer to make sure it's installed, at $100,000—plus training and downtime between the time you order and the time when everything's up, tested, and running. Let's look at this a little differently to help meet our goals."

Between the PE folks and our team, we brought our knowledge to help the CEO see the bigger picture. We convinced them to institute a wage that attracted the people they needed. Within eight weeks, they were fulfilling their demand, and earning $1.5 million in extra profit for $200,000 in cost. If they had taken the other approach, it would have taken six months to ramp up to full capacity, and their costs would have been higher. Question: If your response to keeping up with demand is simply to buy more equipment and you only use 70 percent of its capacity, when does it end? The answer is, it ends when the competitor does it better for less and encroaches on your market share.

Here is a great example of how a bigger-picture perspective can work for an entrepreneurial business owner who (full disclosure) is a personal favorite of mine ...

My sister, Caryn O'Sullivan, started her own window-dressing company in 2007. By 2020, Drapery Street had grown to $2 million in sales, employed nine people, and built a vibrant market position with interior designers and high-end homeowners.

And she was exhausted.

Caryn was personally responsible for 95 percent of their sales and also worked closely with the installers to make sure every job was done well. So, it made sense that she thought about selling the company—she just could not keep this up anymore and be present for her family and live her life.

Here was the challenge: Selling a company that is so heavily dependent on the owner would not only reduce the value of Drapery Street to a potential buyer, they would require her to stay on for years to stabilize the business. This was not her intended plan. Caryn retained a business succession coach to help her increase the value of the company and prepare it for sale.

Over the next three years Caryn:

- Hired a sales coach to develop her team.
- Adopted the Enterprise Operating System (EOS).

- Developed eight key processes which addressed everything from sales, quoting and invoicing, to scheduling installations, and quality control.

Let's park at the "succession planning coach" place for a moment: Do you think it was crazy for her to spend thousands of dollars on a coach? Why didn't she just sell more? Well, Caryn had her eye firmly on the size of the prize, clearly identified the problem she wanted to solve, and brought together the resources to make it happen.

An interesting thing happened. Caryn was motivated to go on this success path because she was so stressed and tired she wanted to sell. However, once she implemented these practices, she realized she no longer needed or wanted to sell. She loved her work and her company and now had more time to realize and relish it.

In May of 2024 as Caryn and I sat on our family farm's deck, she made the most amazing statement: *"Drapery Street is now my hobby."* In four years, she went from personally driving 95 percent of sales to less than 10 percent. She has a VP of Operations who develops their sewing, installation, and warehouse operation teams. They have instituted all eight key processes which are followed by everyone.

Caryn changed her life by thinking bigger and doing it right. Not only did she dramatically increase the value of her company, she made it easier to lead. Now, she is able to think. She is able to focus on strategy. She is able to go to Portugal for a month when she likes!

I am so proud of my sister! And I get to share this great example of how an early-stage company successfully evolved into a stable, sustainable company with solid positioning for whatever next step it chooses to take.

The "Virtuous Cycle"
of continuous improvement

Here is what I want you to know: **The strategic way to use this book is not only to improve your performance today, but also to create a culture of continuous improvement—toward a more mature organization that enjoys shocking and ethical profit.**

Use the opportunities to improve that we identified in Sections I and II to *give your team limitless cycles of small improvements.*

Your action plan is not only about demonstrating results early. The overarching goal is to make sure this plan leads to the final solution or final design: **the future state you set out to achieve.** It lays the framework for you to continue to "plan, do, check, and act" each initiative, and those habits become second nature to your people, embedded in a problem-solving culture.

The beauty is that you rinse and repeat this model for each improvement or change you envision for the company. It becomes part of your business model and your organizational culture.

All the while, you're making improvements that fund themselves, increase profits, boost the value of your company, pave the proven path to a future state of potential succession or sale, and move yourself into the roles of developer of leaders, advisor, and visionary. It's a multi-win model!

A word about organizational culture: *Culture is like happiness.* It is at its best and most real when it is the outcome of daily behavior, rather than an intentional strategy which *mimics* a desired culture. As we chase happiness, we often become inwardly focused and substitute thrills for joy. Activities or acquisitions designed to "bring happiness" eventually wear off. Serving others brings happiness almost by accident. The same is true for culture. The sustainable culture evolves naturally from day-to-day behavior, not only from policies and platitudes detailed in a manual that gathers dust on a virtual shelf.

> **As you develop the standard operating procedure of solving problems and serving others, you will end up with a problem-solving culture and an environment where everyone will love to work!**

How to start? It's simple. As the leader, find an opportunity to say to one of your people: "You own this, [Bob]. I've got your back. Let me know what you need, and let's talk Friday about what you got done and where you're going."

That's how you start the Virtuous Cycle—one by one, team by team, department by department, plant by plant. You start entrusting people to solve problems themselves. You teach them to fish. To do it with your authority and support, but not your involvement.

What does "ethical" have to do with profit?

The term "ethical" was essential for me to include in the title of this book. By ethical I do mean the typical running of a business that adheres to legal, safety, and workplace regulations, and standards—but to me, it's so much more!

I believe ethical profit is sustainable financial gain achieved by leaders who prioritize well-being, dignity, and happiness for all stakeholders—employees, customers, and communities. True success comes from relationships based on trust, fairness, and mutual respect. Profit is not only about money but also about the positive impact on people's lives and the joy of contributing to a better world.

Bob Chapman in his presentation for MindSpring's, "Everybody Matters," expresses it best in this story, excerpted here:

Bob and his team were planning to hold a management meeting in their Green Bay operation, when he received an email: "Bob, you might be aware that a group of our team members just went through a large project in the plant to improve and employ continuous improvement ideas. You might want to walk out and recognize 'em." Bob replied, "Why don't you invite them into the management meeting in the morning and we'll let them share their experience with all of us."

So, at 7:00 a.m. the next morning, these three gentlemen stood before the executive management meeting, and shared the achievements of the project. They had improved quality, cut lead time, reduced inventory financially, everything was shifted on time—a great report on all the numbers, performance, and profits.

Afterward, as Bob relates it, "I was blessed with a thought to ask this one gentleman, 'Kenneth, how did this affect your life?' His answer was, 'I'm talking to my wife more.'"

Not the answer expected by anyone!

Kenneth, a supervisor, went on to say how it had felt before to be part of an organization where you go in every day, and you're told what to do. People don't ask you what you think. You get ten things right and you don't hear a word, but you get one thing wrong, and you never hear the end of it. "Do you know what it feels like to go home at night from that environment?" He said, "You don't feel very good about yourself, and when you don't feel very good about yourself, you're not very nice to your wife."

However, since the company has embraced people-centric leadership and the idea of continuous improvement, Kenneth has experienced the chance to be asked to contribute his ideas and gifts to make things better. His role as supervisor feels much improved.

Because this has happened, he goes home every night feeling valued and better about himself. "And when I go home feeling better about myself, I find I'm nicer to my wife. And believe it or not, when I'm nicer to my wife, she talks to me."

The company became more profitable; that's why leadership started the project. What they appreciated about it afterward was that they accomplished their goals, and their people felt valued, fulfilled, and happy. AND they wanted to stay with the company—engaged, productive, and proud of the role they played in the company's success.

> **To me, this is the essence of ethical profit—better still, joyful profit!**

When you take yourself out of the everyday operations and minutiae of your company, you're not only freeing yourself up for other things that are important to you, you're also giving a gift to your people. The impact you can have on people's lives at this level is immeasurable. Well, it's quantitative in terms of higher productivity, engagement, innovation, attendance, longevity with the organization, leadership development within, and other cost-saving outcomes. But qualitatively? You can never fully measure the positive impact and rewards people experience.

One thing I have learned in my decades working with companies is that pure cost cutting and harsh cultures simply do not produce stable, growing profits. They will help you hit a quarter and maybe even a decade, but that streak will end.

I know I am not telling you anything new. Yet I have seen that for some CEOs, this is a novel idea when a company is stuck in the weeds of getting the job done, putting out fires, playing an endless game of Whack-a-Mole, silo thinking and "command" leadership style.

When a client hires us, it is usually because they have pain around a specific problem and simply want to become more profitable. After the project, what they talk about most is not only the financial results, but also the impact the changes had on their people.

The ideas in this book should confirm that you can design your company to run through a Lean virtuous cycle of continuing improvement, with a problem-solving culture in which people are heard, respected, appreciated, and developed into leaders.

> *"The final test of a leader is that he leaves behind him*
> *in other men the conviction and the will to carry on."*
> —Walter Lippmann, *American journalist*

The real value of a leader is what happens after they leave. If you commit to developing leaders, your company will thrive forever. You keep giving people clarity, visibility, direction, and encouragement. You maintain an environment where everyone on the team is enthusiastically moving toward the same goal, rowing in sync toward the same vision.

Circling back to the very beginning of this book, your company continues to look for hidden risk and Black-Gold value which leads to opportunities to do many small projects, each one providing ROI and teaching your team how to develop leaders. You yield huge improvements that continue to mature your company through Shocking Profits and ethical, joyful success!

> **My sincere hope for you is that YOU DO NOT use this book to drive Shocking Profit.**
>
> **My hope is that your team does.**

Work With Tim Van Mieghem

IF YOU'RE INTERESTED IN REACHING out to Tim Van Mieghem, the author of Shocking Profit, or if you would like to work with him, you can contact him through The ProAction Group. Tim is a partner at The ProAction Group, and he is always open to connecting with individuals who are passionate about improving their business operations and achieving remarkable results.

You can contact Tim and learn more about The ProAction Group at www.proactiongroup.com

You can contact Tim and access Go Deeper Resources for Shocking Profit at www.shockingprofit.com

You can also reach out to Tim directly at Tim@proactiongroup.com

Acknowledgments

I WOULD LIKE TO THANK to my incredible friends, coworkers, and colleagues who have contributed to the creation of this book.

First and foremost, my deepest thanks to Sarah Victory for developing the vision of this book with me. Your creativity and insight have been invaluable.

To Bettyanne Green, your tireless efforts and patience in writing and editing this book have been extraordinary. Your dedication has truly brought this project to life. And you made it fun!

April Gallelli, thank you for your unwavering patience and support during the writing process. Your encouragement motivated me, and your edits kept it real.

I am immensely grateful to Carolyn Henson and Greg Bashford for their extra work and support in running ProAction while I focused on writing this book. Your commitment and hard work have been crucial. I always knew you had my back.

A special thanks to Tom Frey and Mark Panico for their insights, which are shamelessly copied in this book. Your wisdom and experience have greatly enriched the content.

Lastly, I want to express my appreciation to the clients who invited me into their companies. Your trust and collaboration have provided the real-world experiences that form the foundation of this book.

Thank you all for your contributions and support.

Appendix

At the time of this printing, here are the items you can find at www.shockingprofit.com. We will add new materials, tools, and content, so go and explore!

- The Shocking Profit EBITDA Improvement Tool /Model

- The Turn and Earn Benchmark Summary

- The Top 10 Indicators of Hidden Risk and Value

- Copies of the Segmentation Charts

- An example of a Weekly Update form (used by the implementation teams)

- Hints on writing an effective Executive Summary / Business Case

- A deeper dive on The Five Whys problem-solving tool

- Maturity Model

- Monitoring Employee Engagement

Shocking Profit Glossary

A Customers: The group of customers that make up the top 80% of a company's revenue.

A-3 Problem Solving: A structured problem-solving and continuous improvement approach, originated by Toyota. "A-3" refers to the size of paper the team uses to document the definition, relevant data, analysis, solutions, and action plan related to the problem.

A-3 Report: An A-3 report guides the dialogue and analysis. It identifies the current situation, the nature of the issue, the range of possible countermeasures, the best countermeasure, the means (who will do what when) to put it into practice, and the evidence that the issue has actually been addressed. (Lean Institute)[28]

B and C Customers: B customers make up 15% of a company's revenue and C customers make up 5% of a company's revenue.

Black Swan Event: Something that happens despite the fact that people thought it could not happen. (Cambridge Dictionary)[29]

BOM (Bill of Materials): A document showing a list of all the materials and parts that are needed to produce something. (Cambridge Dictionary)[30]

Closed-Loop System: Refers to a Plan, Do, Check, and Act (PDCA) cycle. Think of a company that quotes new business. The quote defines the costs, steps, specifications, and time frame to provide a good or service. In a closed loop system, the team would use the quote as their plan, after completing (doing) the job, then compare the actual outcome against the quote (checking it). When there is a gap between the quote and the outcome, the team will conduct problem-solving sessions to correct the quoting and/or execution processes as needed.

Continuous Improvement (CI): A philosophy and set of principles that focuses on making small, incremental changes to processes, systems, and activities in order to continuously improve them. (Lean Institute)[31]

CRM (Customer Relationship Management): Software that helps organize, manage, and analyze customer interactions.

Cycle Time: The time required to produce a part or complete a process, as timed by actual measurement. (Lean Institute)

Direct Report: An employee whose position at work is directly below that of another person, and who is managed by that person (Cambridge Dictionary) [32]

E&O (Excess and Obsolete Inventory): Inventory that is no longer needed and/or outdated.

EBITDA (Earnings Before Interest, Taxes, Depreciation, and Amortization): A measure of a company's overall financial performance. It is often used to estimate the cash flow produced by the organization and ignores the interest on the debt the owner may have used to acquire the company.

Elastic (vs. inelastic) Pricing: When a good or service has elastic pricing the demand for the item changes when you change the price. When a good has inelastic pricing, changing the price will not immediately drive a change in consumer decisions.

E-Mod Rate: Experience Modifier Rate; a factor used by insurance companies to determine the cost of workers' compensation insurance based on the company's claim history. A rating over 1.0 indicates that the insurance provider considers the company to have a higher risk profile than the typical company in their industry.

FIFO (First In, First Out): The principle and practice of maintaining precise production and conveyance sequence by ensuring that the first part to enter a process or storage location is also the first part to exit. (Lean Institute)[33]

First Pass Yield (FPY): The measurement of products or services that are completed the first time around without any corrections.

Gemba: The Japanese term for "actual place," often used for the shop floor or any place where value-creating work actually occurs. (Lean Institute)[34]

Irregular Activity: Any behavior, transaction, or pattern that falls outside of ethical, normal, or expected operations. This can include unusual spending, unexpected changes in performance, or actions that may indicate errors, fraud, or non-compliance with policies.

Job Shop: A type of manufacturing process where small batches of a variety of custom products are made. Each product may require a different setup and sequence of operations. Job shops are known for flexibility and handling specialized or one-of-a-kind orders. The opposite of a job could be an assembly line that produces volumes of the same or similar products.

Kaizen: A Japanese word that means "continuous improvement". Kaizen aims to make small, incremental improvements in processes and systems, leading to significant long-term benefits. (Lean Institute)[35]

Kanban System: A signaling device that gives authorization and instructions for the production or withdrawal (conveyance) of items in a pull system. (Lean Institute)[36]

KPI (Key Performance Indicator): Measurements that demonstrate how well a company is achieving specific company objectives.

Lagging Indicators: Metrics that reflect past performance and outcomes,

Leading Indicators: Metrics that predict future performance and outcomes.

Lean Manufacturing: Minimizing waste and improving production.

LTL (Less Than Truckload): Combined smaller shipments to fill one truck.

Make vs. Buy Analysis: An evaluation of whether it is more cost-effective to produce a product in-house or purchase it from an external supplier.

Metrics: Quantitative measures used to assess performance, efficiency, and progress toward goals.

MRP (Material Requirements Planning): A production planning, scheduling, and inventory control system used to manage manufacturing processes.

PDCA Cycle: Plan, Do, Check, Act; An improvement cycle based on the scientific method of proposing a change in a process, implementing the change, measuring the results, and taking appropriate action.

PE (Private Equity): Investment funds that buy and restructure companies that are not publicly traded. Think of PE firms like you might think of a real estate developer who might buy a home in order to improve it and then sell it at a profit. PE firms are like real estate developers applied to companies.

Perpetual Inventory System: An inventory management system that continuously tracks inventory levels and updates them in real-time.

Product Mix: All the different products and services a company sells.

ROI (Return on Investment): A measurement of profitability

S&OP (Sales and Operations Planning): A plan that aligns all aspects including financial, supply, and demand.

Schedule Attainment: How closely a project is aligning with the planned upon schedule.

Segmentation Analysis: Dividing a market or customer base into groups based on specific criteria.

SKU (Stock Keeping Unit): A unique code for each product.

Takt Time: A calculation of the available production time divided by customer demand. (Lean Institute)

Throughput: Refers to the amount of material, services, or items passing through a system or process.

Value Stream Map (VSM): A diagram of every step involved in the material and information flows needed to bring a product from order to delivery. It is a fundamental tool used in continuous improvement to identify and eliminate waste.

Work in Progress (WIP): Items that are in the process of being produced but are not yet completed.

Workarounds: Temporary solutions or adjustments made to bypass problems or inefficiencies in a system or process. Often a workaround is intended to circumvent a problem without eliminating the problem.

Yield: The percentage of products or services that meet quality standards and are completed successfully.

About the Author

TIM VAN MIEGHEM IS A Founding Partner of The Pro-Action Group, an operational consulting firm specializing in helping middle-market companies, family-owned businesses, and private equity firms to identify and unlock hidden value. With more than 30 years of hands-on expertise in manufacturing, distribution, and supply chain management, Tim brings a proven track record of turning overlooked inefficiencies into measurable profit.

Prior to founding The ProAction Group in 1995, Tim worked in operational consulting at Arthur Andersen and a boutique supply chain consulting firm. A Certified Public Accountant with a BS in Accounting from Marquette University, Tim has served on the boards of ACME Metal Coatings, Automated Business Machines, and De-Wayne's Quality Metal Coatings.

He is also the host of the *Shocking Profit Podcast*, the author of *Implementing Supply Chain Partnerships*, and the creator of The ProAction Group's proprietary 9-Box Inventory and Pricing Tool. Driven by a passion for sustainable value creation and ethical leadership, Tim believes every company is sitting on a treasure trove of opportunity—if they know where to look.

To learn more or contact Tim directly, visit www.proactiongroup.com or https://www.shockingprofit.com. Follow Tim and The ProAction Group on **LinkedIn** for insights into unlocking your company's hidden profit.

Reviews

"Tim Van Mieghem's 'Shocking Profit' is a masterclass in uncovering hidden value and driving ethical profit."
—Gino Wickman, Author of Traction & Shine, Creator of EOS®

"This book's an eye-opener. After 40 years as a global sales and marketing consultant, I was SHOCKED by Tim's examples of finding massive profits for clients, often right in plain sight."
—Orvel Ray Wilson, CSP, Co-author of Guerrilla Selling,
The Guerilla Group, https://guerrillagroup.com/

"A great roadmap for the due diligence owners should do consistently to unlock 'Shocking Profits' and capture the value for themselves."
—Mark Panico, Principal, Following Seas Business Consulting,
https://www.linkedin.com/in/mark-panico/

"Tim Van Mieghem delivers a powerful, practical roadmap for driving ethical growth and lasting success. His seven secrets reveal how to find, keep, and grow exceptional leaders while uncovering the hidden value inside any organization. A must-read for rising executives eager to create real value and for board members committed to helping companies thrive and prosper."
—Bob Hund, Operating Partner, HCI Equity Partners,
https://www.hciequity.com/

"Business at its core is problem-solving—that's where Shocking Profit steps in. This book shines a light on the blind spots that hold organizations back and reveals untapped value hiding in plain sight. What makes the book stand out is its balance between strategy and practicality. It's packed with real-world examples, proven processes, measurable tools, and frameworks that make the ideas not just inspiring but actionable. Shocking Profit is a guide to cultivating awareness, spotting hidden opportunities, and transforming challenges into growth. If you want to sharpen your vision as a leader and uncover profit that's hiding in your blind spots, this book is a must-read."
—Elaine Damschen, Former President,
Mainstream Electric, Heating, Cooling, & Plumbing,
www.ElaineDamschen.com, and Author of Made in Vietnam

"Shocking Profit is a treasure trove of insights on leadership and organizational success. Tim Van Mieghem's practical steps for uncovering hidden value and fostering a problem-solving culture make this book invaluable for any organization."
—Eric Larson, Managing Partner, Tilia, https://tiliallc.com/

"Shocking Profit by Tim Van Mieghem is a practical and engaging guide that reveals how businesses can uncover hidden value, increase profitability, and create leadership transformation. I wish I had read this book earlier in my career. The information is well presented and totally practical—ideas you can put to work right away. The book's structure—Awareness, Acceptance, and Action—offers a clear roadmap for leaders to unlock growth without massive investments. This is a book to visit over and over again. Its message is powerful and so very helpful."
—Gary Fretwell. #1 International Best Selling Author of Embracing Retirement: Discovering Your Fulfilling Second Act, Speaker

"Shocking Profit" shows business owners how to unlock the hidden value in their businesses today. For companies scared of change, it provides the roadmap to successfully navigate and implement impactful changes that will engage employees and drive better results. This book contains the roadmap, stories, and strategies necessary to drive changes that not only impact the business results, but also change employees' lives. It shows how engaging employees at all levels of the company creates a culture of decision makers, change implementors, and accountability partners in the business results. It is a must-read for any business owner who wants to create a self-sufficient business that can run without their everyday direction or a business that is ready to sell at any time. A must read for any business owner looking to get their time back and stop letting their business run them."

—Debi Corrie, Founder, Acumaxum, LLC, www.acumaxum.com

Endnotes

1   *The Beverly Hillbillies.* Television series, directed by Penelope Spheeris, created by Paul Henning, featuring Buddy Ebsen, Irene Ryan, Donna Douglas, Max Baer Jr., et al. CBS, .https://www.imdb.com/title/tt0055662/

Song Reference
Henning, Paul. *The Ballad of Jed Clampett.* Performed by *Flatt & Scraggs.* Capitol Records, 1962.
Theme song for *The Beverly Hillbillies* (1962–1971)

2   *Star Trek.* Television series, created by Gene Roddenberry, September 8, 1966–June 3. NBC, 1969.

3   **McCrory, Paul.** "Smelling Salts," *British Journal of Sports Medicine* 40, no. 8 (2006): 659–660, https://doi.org/10.1136/bjsm.2006.029710

4   Usain St. Leo Bolt (born August 21, 1986) is a retired Jamaican sprinter widely regarded as the greatest sprinter of all time. He is the only athlete to win gold medals in both the 100–meter and 200–meter races at three consecutive Olympic Games (2008, 2012, and 2016). Bolt still holds the world records in the 100 meters (9.58 seconds) and 200 meters (19.19 seconds), achievements that earned him global fame and the nickname "Lightning Bolt"

5   Bentson, Steve. "Bio." The ProAction Group, https://www.proactiongroup.com/_files/ugd/6ab51d_f078c242834b44339a4f1cb670686af3.pdf. Accessed 22 Sept. 2025.

6   Drucker, Peter F. *The Effective Executive: The Definitive Guide to Getting the Right Things Done.* HarperBusiness, 1967.

7   Connolly, Paul. "The Forgotten Story of … Franz Stampfl," *Bring Back the Mile*, May 29, 2013. https://bringbackthemile.com/news/detail/the_forgotten_story_of_…_franz_stampfl

8   Shakespeare, William. "Sonnet 116". In *The Sonnets*, edited by Katherine Duncan-Jones. Arden Shakespeare, 1997..

9   https://www.proactiongroup.com/_files/ugd/6ab51d_1a0c7ec54b-6b4a4f8b4d06dd18ac8f90.pdf

10 "Getting Started with Lean Accounting. How Does it Work?" *SixSigma.us*, April 23, 2024. https://www.6sigma.us/lean-six-sigma-articles/lean-accounting/

11 Berg, Yehuda. *The Power of the Kabbalah: Technology for the Soul.* Kabbalah Publishing, 2006.

12 *Risky Business.* Directed by Paul Brickman. The Geffen Film Company, 1983.

13 *Still Alice.* Directed by Richard Glatzer, screenplay written by Wash Westmoreland. Sony Pictures Classics, 2014.

14 "American Cancer Society, Cancer Facts & Figures 2022." *American Cancer Society*, n.d. https://www.cancer.org/research/cancer-facts-statistics/all-cancer-facts-figures/cancer-facts-figures-2022.html

15 Garcia, Jon. "Common pitfalls in transformations: A conversation with Jon Garcia." *McKinsey & Company*, March 29, 2022. https://www.mckinsey.com/capabilities/transformation/our-insights/common-pitfalls-in-transformations-a-conversation-with-jon-garcia

16 Byerly, Joe. "The Janitor Who Helped Put a Man on the Moon," *The Green Notebook.* November 4, 2017. https://fromthegreennotebook.com/2017/11/04/the-janitor-who-help-put-a-man-on-the-moon/

17 Brown, Brené. "Clear Is Kind. Unclear Is Unkind," *Brené Brown*, October 15, 2018. https://brenebrown.com/articles/2018/10/15/clear-is-kind-unclear-is-unkind/

18 EOS Methodology, EOS, https://www.eosworldwide.com/

19 "Newton's First Law of Motion," *The Physics Classroom*, 2025, https://www.physicsclassroom.com/class/newtlaws/Lesson-1/Newton-s-First-Law

20 https://www.linkedin.com/in/mark-panico/

21 "Statistical Six Sigma Definition: What It Means for Your Production Line," *iSixSigma*, November 7, 2024, https://www.isixsigma.com/new-to-six-sigma/statistical-six-sigma-definition/

22 "Job Switching," *I Love Lucy*. Television series, written by Jess Oppenheimer, Madelyn Davis, Bob Carroll Jr., directed by William Asher. Season 2, episode 1, aired September 15, 1952.

23 "PDCA Cycle – What is the Plan-Do-Check-Act Cycle?" *ASQ (American Society for Quality)*, n.d. https://asq.org/quality-resources/pdca-cycle

24 Shook, John. *Managing to Learn: Using the A3 Management Process to Solve Problems, Gain Agreement, Mentor and Lead.* Lean Enterprise Institute, 2008.

25 "In most organizations, problems are not viewed as opportunities for improvement, but as failures, and thus are hidden rather than addressed. Problem Solving the Toyota Way," *Toyota Management System*, May 26, 2020, https://www.ineak.com/problem-solving-the-toyota-way/

26 Yoshino, Isao. "How the A3 Came to Be Toyota's Go-To Management Process for Knowledge Work," *Lean Enterprise Institute*, August 2, 2016, https://www.lean.org/the-lean-post/articles/how-the-a3-came-to-be-toyotas-go-to-management-process-for-knowledge-work-intro-by-john-shook/

27 Clancy, Tom. *The Hunt for Red October.* Berkley Publishing, 2010.

28 Lean Enterprise Institute, "A3 Report," *Lean Lexicon*, n.d. https://www.lean.org/lexicon-terms/a3-report/

29 "Black Swan event", Cambridge Dictionary, accessed August 14, 2025, https://dictionary.cambridge.org/dictionary/english/black-swan

30 "Bill of Materials", Cambridge Dictionary, accessed August 14, 2025, https://dictionary.cambridge.org/dictionary/english/bill-of-materials

31 Lean Enterprise Institute, "Continuous Improvement" *Lean Lexicon*, accessed August 16, 2025, https://www.lean.org/lexicon-terms/continuous-improvement/.

32 "Direct Report", Cambridge Dictionary, accessed August 14, 2025, https://dictionary.cambridge.org/dictionary/english/direct-report

33 Lean Enterprise Institute, "First In, First Out (FIFO)," *Lean Lexicon*, n.d. https://www.lean.org/lexicon-terms/first-in-first-out-fifo/

34 Lean Enterprise Institute, "Gemba," *Lean Lexicon*, n.d., https://www.lean.org/lexicon-terms/gemba/

35 Lean Enterprise Institute, "Kaizen," *Lean Lexicon*, n.d., https://www.lean.org/lexicon-terms/kaizen/

36 Lean Enterprise Institute, "Kanban," *Lean Lexicon*, n.d. https://www.lean.org/lexicon-terms/kanban/